THE LOVE OF FOUR COLONELS

COURT THEATRE SCENE IN CASTLE

photo by John Erwin

The Love of Four Colonels

A PLAY IN TWO ACTS

by

PETER USTINOV

DRAMATISTS PLAY SERVICE · INC.
New York
[1953]

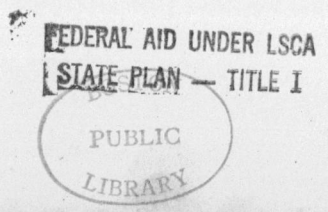

Copyright, 1953, by Peter Ustinov
English Edition, Copyright, 1951, by Peter Ustinov

CAUTION: Professionals and amateurs are hereby warned that THE LOVE OF FOUR COLONELS, being fully protected under the copyright laws of the United States of America, the British Empire, including the Dominion of Canada, and all other countries of the Copyright Union, is subject to a royalty. All rights, including professional, amateur, motion picture, recitation, lecturing, public readings, radio broadcasting, television, and the rights of translation into foreign languages, are strictly reserved.

Inquiries regarding *professional* rights for all countries (*except the United States and Canada*) should be addressed to Film Rights Ltd., 113/117 Wardour Street, London, W.1, England. Inquiries for *professional* rights in the *United States and Canada* should be addressed to MCA Artists Ltd., 598 Madison Avenue, New York 22, N. Y. (acting in association with Film Rights Ltd.)

Inquiries concerning *amateur* rights for performances *outside* of the *United States and Canada* should be addressed to English Theatre Guild Ltd., 75 Berwick Street, London, W.1, England.

The *amateur* acting rights of THE LOVE OF FOUR COLONELS in the *United States and Canada* are controlled exclusively by the DRAMATISTS PLAY SERVICE, INC., 14 East 38th Street, New York 16, N. Y., without whose permission in writing no *amateur* performance of it in such territory may be made.

SOUND EFFECT RECORDS

The following sound effect records, which may be used in connection with this play, can be obtained through the Dramatists Play Service, Inc., at $2.30 each, which price includes packing and shipping.

No. 5005 Church bell
No. 5182 Thunder in distance
No. 5019 Trumpets

NOTE ON MUSIC

As this book goes to press, the original incidental music to be used in connection with this play is not available. Plans in connection with this music are being formulated, and an announcement will be made later on.

The present text of this play conforms literally to the American production. A few changes were made in preparation for this production, which are carried out with the author's consent.

For Richard E. Myers of New York

THE LOVE OF FOUR COLONELS was first produced by Linnit and Dunfee Ltd. (by arrangement with Bronson Albery) at Wyndham's Theater in London, May 23, 1951. It was produced by John Fernald, and the settings were designed by Fanny Taylor. Incidental music was by Antony Hopkins. The cast was as follows:

English Cast

COLONEL DESMOND DE S. RINDER-SPARROW	Colin Gordon
COLONEL WESLEY BREITENSPIEGEL	Alan Gifford
COLONEL AIME FRAPPOT	Engene Deckers
COLONEL ALEXANDER IKONENKO	Theodore Bikel
THE MAYOR OF HERZOGENBURG	Paul Hardtmuth
THE WICKED FAIRY	Peter Ustinov
THE GOOD FAIRY	Gwen Cherrell
THE BEAUTY	Moira Lister
MRS. BREITENSPIEGEL	Patricia Jessel
MME. FRAPPOT	Diana Graves
MRS. RINDER-SPARROW	Mary Hignett
MME. IKONENKO	Mona Lilian

The play was produced in the United States, in a somewhat modified form, at the Sam S. Shubert Theater in New York, by the Theater Guild and Aldrich & Myers. It was staged by Rex Harrison and scenery and costumes were by Rolf Gerard. Karl Nielsen was production stage manager. The cast was as follows:

American Cast

COLONEL WESLEY BREITENSPIEGEL	Larry Gates
COLONEL DESMOND DE S. RINDER-SPARROW	Robert Coote
COLONEL AIME FRAPPOT	George Voskovec
COLONEL ALEXANDER IKONENKO	Stefan Schnabel
MAYOR OF HERZOGENBURG	Reginald Mason
THE MAN (Wicked Fairy)	Rex Harrison
DONOVAN (Good Fairy)	Leueen MacGrath
BEAUTY	Lilli Palmer
Chamberlain	Reginald Mason

IT SHOULD BE CAREFULLY NOTED that the cast in the English production of this play differs considerably in some respects from that of the American production. Since the text printed in this book is that of the American version, the cast of the American production is the one to be followed here.

The characters of Mrs. Breitenspiegel, Mrs. Rinder-Sparrow, Mme. Frappot and Mme. Ikonenko do not appear in the American version and are not in the present text.

The same actor who plays the Mayor plays the Chamberlain.

The Play Service hereby acknowledges with grateful thanks the friendly help of Mr. Karl Nielsen, production stage manager of the American production for his continuous help in preparing the present text.

ACT ONE

ACT ONE

Scene 1

The offices of the Allied Military Administration at Herzogenburg, a village in the Hartz Mountains, disputed by Britain, France, America, and Russia after the Great War of 1939-45. As a consequence of this dispute on a high level, this innocent and charming spot is cursed with an abundance of Colonels, charged by their governments to carry on the friction on an intimate, domestic level. The scene of the battleground is a drab room giving every evidence of near-destruction, but rendered habitable by a liberal dispensation of plywood, cardboard, and asbestos. The furnishing is functional as only military interior decoration can be. There is a trestle-table, C., four chairs, a few ingenious filing systems in cupboardlike containers. The walls are covered with old notices, all of them either urgent or important. There is also a large photograph of a naked woman being coy with a beach ball, a drawing of a bulldog with young, a reproduction of an Utrillo street-scene, and a framed portrait of Joseph Stalin. The window at the back gives over a forest. The upper turrets of a castle can be dimly perceived rising from the jungle. Door U.L. and dummy door R.

As curtain rises Colonel Wesley Breitenspiegel is lying back dangerously in his chair, his feet on the table, smoking a cigar. A bald man with rimless glasses. Colonel Desmond de S. Rinder-Sparrow is sitting forward on the very edge of his chair, puffing at a pipe, his eyes glazed in the manner of an empire-builder hynotized by his greatest enemy, the horizon. *There follows the longest pause in theatrical history, toward the end of which the audience should be convinced that the actors have been the victims of some administrative disaster. The pause is terminated after adequate time for embarrassment has elapsed.*

DESMOND. *(Sitting in chair R. of table)* We seem to have run out of conversation.

WESLEY. *(In chair L. of table)* Yeah . . . *(Pause)* Have you ever contemplated suicide?

DESMOND. *(Deeply interested)* Lord, no. Have you?

WESLEY. No.

DESMOND. I say, old man, you're not . . . I mean . . . ?

WESLEY. *(A little irritated)* What are you so embarrassed about?

DESMOND. Well, I hardly like to say.

WESLEY. Then don't.

DESMOND. You don't have anything rash in mind?

WESLEY. No. Unless you call playing golf with *you* rash.

DESMOND. That's very far from what I meant. This sudden mention of suicide . . .

WESLEY. Oh, no. Good God, no. My wife would be furious. *(Desmond laughs)* What are you laughing at?

DESMOND. You bringing the wife into it.

WESLEY. My wife's not funny. She's very far from funny. But then I don't go for laughter much. I'm a romantic at heart. *(Desmond laughs again)* What are you snickering at now?

DESMOND. I always imagined a romantic as tall and emaciated, with long hair.

WESLEY. (*Taking feet off table*) Do you mean to say that you haven't even got the imagination to conceive of a short-haired romantic?

DESMOND. I've never given the matter a thought, to tell you the honest truth.

WESLEY. Then it's time you did! You have before you a man who dreams of only one thing—to disobey an order in the most glamorous possible way.

DESMOND. (*Shocked*) Disobey an order?

WESLEY. Yes . . . I'd like to have led the Charge of the Light Brigade against all expert advice.

DESMOND. You'd have to have been a British officer to do that.

WESLEY. You're as possessive as a woman.

DESMOND. I'm quoting facts.

WESLEY. O.K., O.K. I'll leave the Charge of the Light Brigade to you.

DESMOND. I don't particularly want it.

WESLEY. And you grudge me having it?

DESMOND. Oh, you can have it if you like.

WESLEY. (*Facing front*) Now I'm sore. I don't want it any more.

DESMOND. I'm sorry. I didn't mean to be difficult about it.

WESLEY. (*Defiant—turning back to Desmond*) I still have Custer's Last Stand.

DESMOND. Yes, I suppose you have.

WESLEY. Listen, I'll tell you just how romantic I am.

DESMOND. (*Rises, crosses L.C.*) Are you positive you haven't told me before?

WESLEY. You know, you're the one man who's ever made me lose my taste for conversation.

DESMOND. I've always preferred silence myself. (*Picks up magazine from sofa L., looks at it*)

WESLEY. (*Vindictive*) In that case I'm sorry to disappoint you.

DESMOND. I'm used to disappointment, old fellow.

WESLEY. Well, I'm not. My romanticism is entirely personal and selfish. It is, according to my psychiatrist, ingrowing, largely owing to the inadequacy of my father.

DESMOND. (*Turns to Wesley, sits in chair L.C., reading magazine*) He seems to have been adequate enough to bring you into the world.

WESLEY. He was counterbalanced by the overadequacy of my mother, and of a certain Doctor Purkiss.

DESMOND. Was he the family doctor?

WESLEY. In more ways than one.

DESMOND. (*Looks at Wesley*) Good gracious me.

WESLEY. A compromise was reached. My second name is Purkiss.

DESMOND. How very unusual.

THE LOVE OF FOUR COLONELS

WESLEY. My psychiatrist assures me it is absolutely usual, and that it is wrong to conceal such things, as a lack of ventilation alone breeds complexes. Have you a psychiatrist?

DESMOND. In England we can't afford them. Thank God. (*Reads again. Colonel Aimé Frappot enters. He is short and a little sour*) Hello, Aimé.

AIMÉ. Ikonenko not here yet? (*Hangs up hat on back wall peg*)

DESMOND. No sign of him.

AIMÉ. (*Crossing R. of back of table*) The conference should have begun five minutes ago. I hoped I would be late.

DESMOND. (*Smiling*) Not looking forward to it?

AIMÉ. (*Arranging personal effects on table*) Enormously. Last week we all talked in French. I could relax and tell you what I thought of you with no fear of contradiction. (*Gets out cigarette*)

DESMOND. I don't know why we should have to talk French when we all know English.

AIMÉ. (*Crossing L. around in front of table*) It is all a question of honor. English may be more convenient, but it will not be used if there is the chance of the French language being slighted. (*Feels in pocket for a match. Not finding one, goes to Desmond, who is lighting his pipe*) Vous permettez? (*Desmond gives him a light*)

WESLEY. Next week we all have to speak Russian.

AIMÉ. Merci! It's then that Ikonenko pushes all his legislation through, and we get into trouble.

WESLEY. Yeah. The bastard. (*Rises, crosses R. to filing cabinet*)

AIMÉ. He's not a bad fellow.

DESMOND. Clever.

AIMÉ. We mustn't be ungenerous enough to grudge him that.

WESLEY. (*Starting to fix Seidlitz powders from table R.*) After all, we're all clever in our own way.

AIMÉ. (*With a smile and a glance at Wesley*) Yes. (*Crosses to front of C. table*) It's strange how I hate this place, and yet I know in advance I'll be sorry to leave it. (*Sits on table C.*) Have you ever noticed how, in life, hatred is as binding a tie as love? The pathos of leaving a detested school, or a mistress who has begun to bore you?

DESMOND. (*Charming*) Heavens, I always begin to bore them first.

AIMÉ. (*A little disarmed*) I must remember that. It's a perfectly charming remark.

DESMOND. Is it?

WESLEY. (*Pouring Seidlitz powders and mixing with water—drinking part of it*) Why did you go into the Army, Aimé?

AIMÉ. My father said it was the best entrée into politics. He was a man hypnotized by his own mediocrity.

DESMOND. Oh, I say. Those are hard words for anyone to use about his old man. What was he?

AIMÉ. He was Minister of Agriculture for ten minutes in 1912. (*Others laugh. Crosses L. to Desmond*) You know, Desmond, you look like a man who has never had the embarrassment of a choice in his life.

THE LOVE OF FOUR COLONELS 17

DESMOND. (*As Wesley gets folder from file cabinet*) Well, in my case it was a toss-up between the Army and the Church. Luckily there were more vacancies in the Army at that particular moment, so my mind was made up for me. I wasn't very bright, you understand.

AIMÉ. I understand entirely. (*Turns U.R. a step*)

DESMOND. (*Suddenly laughing*) Before you came in, Wesley said he was a romantic.

AIMÉ. I know he is.

DESMOND. Is he?

AIMÉ. (*Crossing U.R.*) Yes. He's a romantic. I'm a realist. And you . . . you're a thoroughly nice fellow. That's why we get on so badly. Think of us for a moment, and reflect on the stupidity of our employers. (*Down C. beside conference table*) We have been here ever since this disputed zone was created, two and a half years ago, and in that time we have decided nothing except that we wish to transfer our headquarters from here to that overgrown palace. (*Gazes at it through widow U.C.*)

WESLEY. (*Places folder he is holding on conference table, gets second folder from filing cabinet*) Hey, I've had the latest reports in from the troops trying to get through to the castle.

AIMÉ. (*U.C. and a step R.*) Any results?

WESLEY. (*Crossing U.C. to Aimé*) No. Lieutenant Coppermaker reports that at first he thought the weeds uprooted during the day were being replaced in some mysterious way by the local population during the night. Now he's convinced the plants are growing together by themselves during the hours of darkness, and suggests finally that Washington should send a man.

DESMOND. Is he going to?

18 THE LOVE OF FOUR COLONELS

WESLEY. If you knew Washington, you'd realize that that is the silliest thing to ask it to do. What I've done is to send Lieutenant Coppermaker to the psychiatrist for a start. (*Starts back toward filing cabinet.*)

AIMÉ. (*Smiles, crossing R. two steps*) You are sceptical because you are a romantic. I, being a realist, am prepared to accept Lieutenant Coppermaker's report.

WESLEY. What do you mean?

AIMÉ. (*Agreeable*) I believe in fairies. (*U.R. of conference table*)

DESMOND. Well, you know, in Ireland—they have those little jobs—

WESLEY. I know, leprechauns. Listen to me—(*Door opens, and Colonel Ikonenko enters, hangs up hat on L. hook, crosses down to L.C. chair, sits. An entirely expressionless man carrying a briefcase. There is an electric silence occasioned by his entrance*) You're late. (*Ikonenko doesn't answer. He just sits at his place, back of table, spreads his papers out, then says*)

IKONENKO. Now *you're* late. (*Desmond throws magazine on table D.L., crosses C., sits chair R. of table. Others all make haste to sit down. Wesley picks up first folder, crosses back of table, sits at L. end*) Colonel Breitenspiegel, I wish to bring to your attention as chairman for this week that I am chairman by rotation next week, and that the official language for the seven days commencing—(*Consults a diary*)—on the 18th will be Russian.

WESLEY. (*Seated L. end of table*) There's no need to rub that in.

AIMÉ. (*Seated beside Ikonenko*) Colonel Ikonenko, may I permit myself the honor of bringing to your kind attention the fact that during the week commencing—(*Consults a diary*)—the 2nd,

THE LOVE OF FOUR COLONELS

that is, eight days after the conclusion of your term as chairman, I shall be in the Chair, and the recognized language will be French.

IKONENKO. That is generally understood.

DESMOND. I trust no one is forgetting that—(*Flicking pages of diary*)—Where are we?—Yes—that on the 25th it's my turn, and we all speak English.

AIMÉ. On behalf of my Government, I agree.

WESLEY. There's no need to put all this to the vote, I trust?

IKONENKO. (*Secretive*) It may be better.

WESLEY. But good God, we all agree.

IKONENKO. You never know.

WESLEY. Well, I'm against it. It's ridiculous. It's a waste of time.

IKONENKO. I must insist.

WESLEY. In that case, I propose that this committee does not wish to vote on the agreement of the agreement, owing to the redundancy of so doing. Will all in favor of not voting kindly signify their viewpoint in the usual way? (*Wesley, Desmond, and Aimé raise hands and put them down*) Now will all in favor of voting raise their hands? (*Ikonenko lifts hand*) The Committee has voted by a majority of three to one not to vote. (*Ikonenko rises, packs all his documents, crosses U.L., gets hat and leaves room*) Crazy guy.

AIMÉ. He'll be back in a minute.

DESMOND. Extraordinary waste of energy. (*Pause. Ikonenko re-enters, puts hat on rack, replaces all his documents expressionlessly, crosses to his chair, and sits*)

IKONENKO. What is next on the agenda?

WESLEY. You haven't given me much time to look up my notes, have you?

IKONENKO. Is there any report on the state of the castle yet from your subordinate?

WESLEY. Yes. All in good time.

IKONENKO. I have received a report on the situation independently of yours. Lieutenant of the 3rd Grade Bulganov—

WESLEY. (*Livid*) That is in direct contravention of our agreement that the duty of investigating and clearing the undergrowth surrounding the castle devolved on United States arms.

IKONENKO. (*Firm*) Lieutenant of the 3rd Grade Bulganov's word is above suspicion. He is a Hero of Stalingrad, a Hero of Labor, and holder of the Suvorov Medal of the 2nd Class.

WESLEY. That has nothing to do with it! Lieutenant Coppermaker is an accredited member of the New York Stock Exchange, and an old Princeton alumnus.

AIMÉ. I thought you said he had been sent to the psychiatrist?

WESLEY. (*Faltering—turns away toward audience*) On a social call. The psychiatrist is an old personal friend of his.

AIMÉ. From the Stock Exchange?

WESLEY. Yes. —No, from Princeton. I will begin with Lieutenant Coppermaker's report. Mummum. (*Skips passages which seem irrevelant*) ". . . I am convinced after three days' work on the undergrowth that some botanical phenomenon is restricting our progress. It is clear to anyone with an elementary knowledge of gardening that the reconstruction of the weeds is far

THE LOVE OF FOUR COLONELS

neater and more accurate than could be achieved by human labor. I therefore feel . . ." Mummummummm . . . in a nutshell, that is Lieutenant Coppermaker's report.

IKONENKO. Colonel Breitenspiegel, there is no room in our relationship for nutshells. Why, Colonel Breitenspiegel, were you mumbling?

WESLEY. Red tape, Colonel Ikonenko. Unadulterated military red tape.

IKONENKO. Your attitude is deeply unpleasant to me. Rather than argue with you, I will set you an example. Contrary to the hysteria shown by Lieutenant Coppermaker, the report of Lieutenant of the 3rd Grade Bulganov is both brilliant and to the point. (*Opens document*) Mummummummum . . . "It is easy to understand that the lack of progress in the clearing of the undergrowth is due to (1) the lack of will to work shown by American soldiers unversed in Socialist doctrine, (2) the consistent sabotage exercised by reactionary diversionists and Fascist hyenas . . . (*Wesley opens his mouth to reply, but is too late*)

DESMOND. Nobody with a working knowledge of the hyena would ever credit it with any political sense.

WESLEY. (*Angry*) Desmond, for God's sake don't interrupt. What was the meaning of all *that* mumbling, Ikonenko? Here's something I want to put to the vote, fellows.

IKONENKO. I object.

WESLEY. I move that this meeting deplores the underhand, surreptitious and dishonest nature of the Soviet tactics on the occasion of the report over the operations to free the castle from its surrounding jungle. Will all those in favor kindly raise their hands? (*Wesley and Desmond raise hands, but Aimé rises and goes toward door. Immediate tension. All half-rise*)

IKONENKO. (*Rising*) Does this move of yours reflect the official French attitude?

AIMÉ. (*U. to door L.*) What? (*Turns back*)

WESLEY. Does this mean a split in the Atlantic Bloc?

AIMÉ. Why?

IKONENKO. I must telegraph Moscow immediately. (*Sits, writes*)

AIMÉ. For what reason?

WESLEY. (*Crossing U.L. to Aimé*) I warn you, Aimé, this action may affect United States Economic Aid.

AIMÉ. What action?

DESMOND. (*Rises, stays at R. end of table*) Remember Verdun, old son—don't let us down now!

AIMÉ. Who am I letting down?

WESLEY. Us. By walking out of the conference now, of all times.

AIMÉ. There comes a time during the day when even the most strongly constituted of us has to leave the room. I'll be back in a minute. (*Aimé goes out. Desmond sits*)

WESLEY. (*Crossing back to Ikonenko*) There are times when nature reasserts herself, Ikonenko, and laughs in the face of all governments. That should be a chastening thought for you.

IKONENKO. The Soviet Government has never attempted to deny the presence of nature in the world. On the other hand, we are pioneers of Socialist-Realism, and the dishonest manner in which Colonel Frappot left the room reflects the mocking and decadent state of contemporary French so-called civilization.

THE LOVE OF FOUR COLONELS

DESMOND. How does a Socialist-Realist—a—a—go to the—?

IKONENKO. I do not understand the question.

WESLEY. What would you have done?

IKONENKO. I should have made my intentions clear.

DESMOND. How terribly embarrassing.

WESLEY. Speaking then as a Socialist-Realist—

IKONENKO. But you are not one.

WESLEY. O.K. Speaking as a—what is it? Pluto-Democrat—

IKONENKO. You condemn yourself!

WESLEY. It's rather fun. I like it. Speaking as one of those, I think Stalin stinks.

IKONENKO. I think the same of Truman.

WESLEY. So do I. I'm a Republican. (*Aimé returns*)

AIMÉ. (*U.L.*) The Mayor is waiting outside . . . did any of you summon him?

WESLEY. (*Turns to Aimé*) I did, yes.

IKONENKO. Without consulting us? (*Starts to pack up his things*)

WESLEY. Have him come in. (*Desmond rises, crosses U.R.C. Wesley says to Ikonenko*) If you walk out now, you'll miss the fun. (*Aimé goes to door, returns with Mayor of Herzogenburg. Very old, very benevolent*) Dr. Busch, why, come right in. (*Shakes hands with him. Crosses behind and to L. of him*)

MAYOR. (*Beaming*) So nice. (*Shakes Wesley's hand*) Oberst Breitenspiegel. Your name I remember, it's a good old German name. (*Aimé crosses R.*)

WESLEY. We're descended from the Counts of Breitenspiegel.

MAYOR. This I didn't know. But once we had, when I was small, a man who was sharpening the knives in the village. He had exactly this name of Breitenspiegel.

WESLEY. Yes . . . well, you know Colonel Frappot.

MAYOR. (*In appalling French*) Mais oui!

AIMÉ. En effet, Monsieur le maire. (*Crosses R.*)

DESMOND. Good evening, Mr. Mayor.

WESLEY. Colonel Rinder-Sparrow.

MAYOR. (*Laughing*) You must forgive it to me. Such a name I can't not so remember. Breitenspiegel—

WESLEY. Colonel Ikonenko. (*Ikonenko doesn't look up*)

MAYOR. (*Determined to make an impression*) **D**a, da, da.

WESLEY. (*Crossing to chair*) Won't you sit down?

IKONENKO. I must make my position clear. I am opposed to your visit here.

MAYOR. Why?

IKONENKO. I was not consulted.

MAYOR. (*Pityingly*) Is that the only reason?

THE LOVE OF FOUR COLONELS 25

WESLEY. Others will occur to him later on. Come on, sit down. Have a cigar? *(Mayor sits chair L.C., hat on floor R. of chair)* Now, Herr Busch, *(Crosses, sits on couch L.)* we'll come straight to the point. Suppose you tell us about the castle.

MAYOR. *(Strange)* I know nothing about it. *(Pauses, taking off gloves)*

IKONENKO. He's bluffing.

WESLEY. But you do know that the weeds around it behave in the strangest way.

IKONENKO. *(Loud)* He knows! He is responsible for it all!

MAYOR. I know it is difficult to reach the castle . . .

WESLEY. Difficult? It's damned impossible!

MAYOR. I have never tried it myself, even though my great-grandfather was once the chamberlain there.

WESLEY. Why not? I should have thought that human inquisitiveness alone would have—

MAYOR. In these parts we know better than to try. We leave it to the others.

AIMÉ. *(Intrigued)* Which others?

MAYOR. *(Puts gloves into hat)* The officials. People like you. There was a Gauleiter who came here eight years ago. He tried to enter, and failed.

DESMOND. Good heavens, we're not in Tibet. What is all this mystery?

MAYOR. Before him, there was an official of the Gestapo who

came here. Once again he tried, and once again he failed. He is now in a lunatic asylum.

WESLEY. A lunatic asylum—why?

IKONENKO. Herr Busch, your attitude, even though it is impossible to understand, does you no credit. I must warn you against the terrible danger of being incomprehensible in the future. I shall give the order tonight for Soviet troops to begin operations for the occupation of the castle at dawn tomorrow, so that it may pass back into the hands of its legitimate owners, the people!

AIMÉ. (*Who has been pacing agitatedly, at R. corner of table, beside Ikonenko*) Mon colonel, I ask you to reconsider your order to your troops.

IKONENKO. Actions are more comprehensible than words!

AIMÉ. And more dangerous.

IKONENKO. The victors must educate the defeated. Our position here has been made ridiculous by (1) the lack of initiative shown by American troops in clearing the undergrowth, and (2) the Wall Street tactics of —

WESLEY. (*Jumping up, crossing to Ikonenko*) I've had enough of this!

DESMOND. (*Jumping up*) May I appeal for some good sound British common sense?

IKONENKO. What have you to say?

DESMOND. (*Crossing L.*) Nothing as yet, but I'm thinking furiously. (*Wesley sits L. of table*)

MAYOR. (*Softly, as he rises*) Dear boys, you are making your-

THE LOVE OF FOUR COLONELS 27

selves ill, and all for such silly reasons. You must take care of yourselves. (*Crosses to Ikonenko*) Are you married, Colonel Ikonenko?

IKONENKO. I do not discuss my affairs in public.

MAYOR. Your wife is an official secret also?

AIMÉ. I am married. We are all married. (*Steps down R. of conference table*)

MAYOR. And are you happy?

AIMÉ. Speaking personally, she is the mother of my children.

MAYOR. And that is all?

AIMÉ. (*Down R. of conference table*) I live with an actress. My wife lives with a transport chief. Apart from that, we are inseparable.

MAYOR. But your children?

AIMÉ. (*Simply*) I love them.

DESMOND. What has all this to do with the castle?

MAYOR. (*Turns to Desmond, L.*) A great deal, Colonel. Have you a wife and a home?

DESMOND. Yes, and three dogs.

MAYOR. And you love them?

DESMOND. Yes, I breed them. Dingos. Wild dogs, you know.

MAYOR. (*Turns to Wesley*) Herr Breitenspiegel is also married?

WESLEY. Don't talk to me. The doctor told me I've got to be free from all worry.

MAYOR. Then, as you all have something worth living for, children, forget the castle. I appeal to you before it's too late!

DESMOND. Too late? Too late for what?

MAYOR. (*Very softly, crossing down L. to Desmond*) . . . All I know is that when I was telling the Gauleiter what I had heard about the castle, the door opened slowly without our noticing it . . . (*Door begins to open slowly*)

AIMÉ. (*Crossing U.L. two steps*) And who came in?

MAYOR. (*His voice filled with wonder*) Nobody . . . (*Ikonenko suddenly laughs*)

IKONENKO. Brilliantly dramatic!

AIMÉ. Who opened that door? (*Wesley crosses U.R. of door, looks out, sees no one, comes back, stands R. of door*)

IKONENKO. The wind.

AIMÉ. (*At window*) Look at the trees. There's no wind today.

MAYOR. (*Turns to face R.—agonized*) Oh, my dear children, change the subject!

AIMÉ. What happened then?

MAYOR. (*Crosses R. two steps*) A bell rang. A terrible cracked **church** bell.

IKONENKO. (*After a pause, triumphant*) Silence! (*A distant church bell rings a discordant note*)

THE LOVE OF FOUR COLONELS 29

MAYOR. (*Vehement—crosses U.R. to C.*) You fools!

AIMÉ (*Crossing to Mayor, shouting*) What happened then? (*The figure of a man [Wicked Fairy] appears silently at door, dressed as a tramp. Enters U.L. He is tall, thin, and he smiles. Mayor expresses the greatest terror, cowers, crosses himself*)

WICKED FAIRY. (*Calm*) Guten Abend, Herr Busch. (*Mayor gets his hat from D.L.*)

MAYOR. Guten Abend . . . (*Runs out L.*)

IKONENKO. (*Rises*) Who are you? Where is your permit?

WICKED FAIRY. I have many permits to do many things, but I can afford to ignore them.

IKONENKO. No, my friend, you cannot afford to ignore them. You may not circulate without a permit, and you may not enter this office without an appointment.

WICKED FAIRY. (*Crossing D.L.C.*) I have an appointment.

IKONENKO. We never make appointments during conference hours.

WICKED FAIRY. All you need to do is look in your appointment book, dear. (*Sits in armchair L.C. Desmond crosses table D.L., picks up appointment book*)

IKONENKO. No use, I know we have no appointments. Now will you kindly leave before I call soldiers.

WICKED FAIRY. Your soldiers are all asleep. I passed them on the way up, sleeping like babies.

IKONENKO. (*Crossing to L.C. chair*) What? You are lying! (*Desmond looks through appointment book*)

WICKED FAIRY. Oh, you nasty man. (*Rises*) What a horrid thing to say! (*Crosses to R., looking about room and at things on wall.*)

DESMOND. (*Who has been fingering appointment book*) I say, it's quite true.

IKONENKO. What?

DESMOND. There is an appointment here.

WESLEY. (*Crossing D.L. to Desmond*) For whom?

DESMOND. I don't know. It's in Russian. (*Aimé crosses D.L. to look at book*)

IKONENKO. Let me see. (*Desmond passes book to him.*) Professor Diabolikov. I did not write this.

DESMOND. It's in your handwriting, old son.

IKONENKO. (*As Desmond takes book, puts it on table D.L.*) Diabolikov. Is that your name?

WICKED FAIRY. (*Crossing back of table C.*) It was a nickname Catherine the Great gave me . . . to please Voltaire. They shared the joke. I never thought it very funny. (*Takes off his scarf, puts it on chair L. of table C.*)

IKONENKO. I must warn you—

WICKED FAIRY. Against the dangers of incomprehensibility. I know. (*Puts hat on table C.*)

IKONENKO. What—? Are you a Russian subject?

WICKED FAIRY. Not predominantly. (*Puts cloak on chair L. of table*)

THE LOVE OF FOUR COLONELS

IKONENKO. I expect a specific answer.

WICKED FAIRY. I expect an intelligent question, duckie. (*At L. end of table*)

DESMOND. I regret to say the fellow's English.

WICKED FAIRY. (*Crossing front of table*) Not unqualifiedly. I'm just talking English because this is the week for talking English. . . . If you had inspired a visit next week, I should have talked Russian with pleasure.

AIMÉ (*Crossing to Wicked Fairy*) How did you know about our ruling?

WICKED FAIRY. (*Sitting in front of table*) How did I know . . . and love . . . Catherine the Great?

AIMÉ. Love?

WICKED FAIRY. In my way . . .

AIMÉ. Vous l'avez aimée . . . ?

WICKED FAIRY. (*In perfect French*) Selon ma façon . . . (*Aimé crosses L., back to Ikonenko*)

IKONENKO. You have not produced a satisfactory permit.

WICKED FAIRY. (*Searching his vast coat*) You really are most difficult to convince. Here you are. Take your permit. —What's this? (*Pulls out a scroll*) Oh, no. This is permission from Nero to taunt the lions before their dinner of gospellers. Here we are. —No. A front-row ticket for Robespierre's execution. A disappointing affair. (*Reclines on table*) The weather was far from perfect. There's a special kind of weather which is ideal for executions, you know—you need an autumn morning, really, to surround the scene with an aura of poetic melancholy, with just enough of an orange sun to catch the blade. For lions, on the other hand, you can't do better than your midsummer heat, in which the poor beasts are torn between an oppressive lethargy and their greed for blood. Such leonine quandaries drag out the agony of the gospellers deliciously. (*Sits up—with a giggle*) But what am I doing, talking about it as though it still went on today? No, alas. (*He sighs*) The taste for limited horror was dissipated. (*Moves a step or two R.*) A decadence set in. (*Turns*) Our love of quality was polluted by a love of quantity. Nowadays we do things on a majestic scale, with guns and bombs and gases, and it's surprising how the human species obeys our every whim in this direction . . . (*Looking at the Colonels*) All dressed up in their little boiler suits, with bits of gold and silver braid to mark the degree of their guilt. (*Laughs*) Oh dear, oh dear . . . (*Crosses U.R.*)

IKONENKO. (*Crossing C.—terrible*) Where is the permit?

WICKED FAIRY. (*Feminine*) Oh, do stop nagging, Sasha! (*Crosses from R. to Ikonenko C.*) I've got it. Look. Signed by you. (*Gives Ikonenko permit*) This man may go anywhere, do anything and say anything at any time. Signed Ikonenko.

IKONENKO. (*His hand trembling*) This permit is a forgery, and is confiscated.

WICKED FAIRY. I don't mind. I've got plenty more. Look, here's the same signed by Stalin, on official paper. (*Ikonenko seizes it*)

IKONENKO. This permit is likewise—

WICKED FAIRY. Do you dare to suggest that this is a forgery, too? (*In terribly accurate and menacing Russian*) Astarojna, Tovarisch Polkovnik! (*He wags a finger*) Astarojna! I may well be an officer of N.K.V.D. (*Crosses below Ikonenko to C. Turns*) You never can be sure.

THE LOVE OF FOUR COLONELS

IKONENKO. The situation is open to review. (*Wicked Fairy crosses to sofa L.*)

WESLEY. What does that mean? (*Counters cross, watches Wicked Fairy*)

IKONENKO. (*Sits sofa L.*) This is a purely Soviet matter.

DESMOND. (*Moves to chair L.C. Knocks out pipe on shoe*) I damn well *hope* it is.

IKONENKO. (*Crosses U.L.C. to back of table*) The conditions in this town are perilous for visitors. I therefore take the liberty of placing you in protective custody until it is safe for you to circulate. (*Rings bell on table*)

WICKED FAIRY. I told you the soldiers were asleep. Nobody will answer the bell.

IKONENKO. We shall see.

WICKED FAIRY. (*Pokes Desmond's foot with stick*) Tobacco, Colonel?

DESMOND. (*Turns to him*) Thank you so much. I only smoke my own brand.

WICKED FAIRY. McPherson's Fine Old Curly Shag. (*Reaches into his pocket*)

DESMOND. How did you know?

WICKED FAIRY. (*Rising, his pouch now out*) It's the only kind I have.

DESMOND. But it's unobtainable outside the Shetland Islands.

WICKED FAIRY. I know. Isn't it a bore! (*Gives Desmond pouch. Crosses below Wesley, L.C., turns. To Wesley*) Colonel, cigar?

WESLEY. I bet you don't have my brand.

WICKED FAIRY. Cherokee Blues?

WESLEY. Well, what do you know! (*Wicked Fairy throws it over*)

WICKED FAIRY. (*In front of table C.*) Mon colonel, Gauloise Bleue?

AIMÉ. (*Pleasant, crossing down in line*) Je ne dirai pas non.

WICKED FAIRY. (*Giving him packet of cigarettes*) Voilà . . . Comrade Colonel—

IKONENKO. I don't smoke.

WICKED FAIRY. I have even catered for you: I have brought you nothing. (*Crosses below table R. Ikonenko presses bell again, viciously*)

DESMOND. I say, I've been thinking.

WICKED FAIRY. (*Crosses to R.*) Yes?

DESMOND. It's just occurred to me . . .

WICKED FAIRY. Yes?

DESMOND. Who are you?

WICKED FAIRY. (*Sighing sadly*) It's a long story.

AIMÉ. (*Looking for match*) How long?

WICKED FAIRY. (*A little surprised*) Very, very long.

AIMÉ. I have no light.

THE LOVE OF FOUR COLONELS

WICKED FAIRY. (*Crossing to C.*) Oh, I'm so sorry. (*Pulls out an enormous and elaborate table light from his robes, which gives a flame like a blowtorch. They all gaze at it in astonishment. With some trepidation Aimé lights his cigarette from it. Pause*)

AIMÉ. (*Crossing R., turns back to Wicked Fairy*) Do you know who I think you are?

WICKED FAIRY. (*R.C.*) No.

AIMÉ. The Devil.

WICKED FAIRY. (*Falsetto*) Who?

AIMÉ. (*Charming*) The Devil.

WICKED FAIRY. Why? Do I look like him?

AIMÉ. I don't know. I've never met him. But he's someone I've always wanted to meet. We have so much in common.

WICKED FAIRY. I'm glad you've never met him, dear, because I've never been told that I look like him before, even by those who know us both very well. (*Sits in chair R. end of table*) I don't want to seem catty, or say anything behind his back which could give offense, because I have the very, very highest regard for him, but I don't think looks are his strong point. Dear me, no.

DESMOND. This is ridiculous. I suppose the next thing you'll be telling us is that you know God.

WICKED FAIRY. (*Sore point*) I always go out of my way to smile at Him, but He *always* cuts me dead.

IKONENKO. (*Crosses to get hat, opens door*) This man is mad. I am going to fetch the soldiers.

WICKED FAIRY. Sorry if I've been boring you about God and the Devil—I beg your pardon, the Devil and God.

IKONENKO. I recognize no such people. (*Stamps out, L., closing door*)

AIMÉ. But then, who are you?

WESLEY. (*Crossing U.L., behind conference table*) He's come straight out of an asylum.

DESMOND. (*Stepping U.L.C.*) How d'you explain all those tricks of his? How d'you explain the tobacco?

WESLEY. (*Behind C. of conference table*) He's a magician who's gone crazy. Yeah, that's it—the guy's a crazy magician.

DESMOND. (*Crossing behind C. of conference table*) It goes deeper than that, I'm afraid, Wesley. This tobacco. It's the genuine article. Marvelous. It takes a lot to convince me, but now . . .

AIMÉ. What has he convinced you of? (*They look at Wicked Fairy fixedly. He becomes coy*)

WICKED FAIRY. You're making my ears tingle, talking about me like that.

WESLEY. (*Taking step toward Wicked Fairy*) Why did you come here?

WICKED FAIRY. In answer to a summons.

WESLEY. Who summoned you?

WICKED FAIRY. I came to take you to the castle.

DESMOND. The castle! (*Ikonenko enters L., closes door*)

IKONENKO. All the soldiers have been drugged! (*Crosses down L.*) This is sabotage and counter-revolutionary activity of the most dangerous sort. (*To Wicked Fairy*) You are under arrest.

WICKED FAIRY. Don't be silly. (*Rises*)

IKONENKO. Stay where you are!

WICKED FAIRY. I want to stretch my legs.

IKONENKO. (*Crosses C. Draws revolver. Shouts*) Stay where you are!

DESMOND. Ikonenko!

WESLEY. Put that away! } (*Together*)

AIMÉ. I forbid it!

WICKED FAIRY. Don't worry about me, dears. (*Approaches Ikonenko*) Now don't make a fool of yourself, there's a love. (*Crosses C. to L. Ikonenko shoots once; twice; then twice again in rapid succession. Wicked Fairy scratches his stomach. Feline*) It's terrible how bullets tickle!

IKONENKO. (*Appalled*) He's alive! (*Drops revolver on floor, collapses onto floor*)

DESMOND. (*Crosses D.L.C. to Wicked Fairy—military*) Explain yourself.

WICKED FAIRY. (*In front of L.C. chair*) Who? . . . Me?

DESMOND. Yes, indeed, sir. Why aren't you dead?

WICKED FAIRY. Why should I be?

DESMOND. Don't sidestep the issue, sir. This is the most inconsiderate behavior. After all, we are in some sense allied to the

Russians, and look what you've done to my friend over there. (*Ikonenko is in a state of collapse*) He's in a perfectly ghastly condition. What you've done, sir, is neither fair nor funny. I can only put it down to lack of breeding. Now, out with it!

WICKED FAIRY. Out with what?

DESMOND. Kindly apologize to Colonel Ikonenko this instant, and if indeed you have drugged the soldiery, I would ask you to bring them to a state of consciousness with all due dispatch.

WICKED FAIRY. I've never been so bullied in all my endless life! Why should I apologize to Ikonenko? He called me names, and I'm very sensitive indeed. (*Shoves Ikonenko's hand from L.C. chair, sits in it*) As for the soldiers, they're asleep, not drugged.

DESMOND. (*Crosses U.L. to door, then crosses D.L.C. to Wicked Fairy*) Then wake them up. If they sleep any longer they'll miss their tea. As for Ikonenko, I must appeal to what honor you have to realize that there's a great difference between an officer doing his duty and a fellow assing around with live bullets inside him and refusing to lie down.

WICKED FAIRY. No, I won't apologize. I'm sulking.

DESMOND. In that case, I have no alternative but to place you under arrest pending investigation. (*To his colleagues, crossing U.C. behind table*) Do you agree with me?

WESLEY. I guess so, but I don't like it. —Say, how do you do it? You'd have had a great future in Chicago in the twenties.

WICKED FAIRY. What are you doing? (*Desmond presses bell on table*)

DESMOND. Ringing for Sergeant Daniels.

WICKED FAIRY. Nobody will answer that bell!

DESMOND. They'll come if I ring.

AIMÉ. Tell us about the castle.

DESMOND. (*Crossing to Ikonenko, lifts him onto sofa L.*) I advise you not to talk to the fellow.

AIMÉ. I want to know. You see, I think we ought to arrest him, but I don't think we can.

WICKED FAIRY. Bravo! The castle? (*Rises, crosses U.L.C.*) Yes, I'll take you there if you're very, very good.

DESMOND. (*Business with Ikonenko—kneeling*) If I go, I go alone.

WICKED FAIRY. (*Turns*) You won't get in. You see, it is not a castle like any other. It is a castle (*Crossing U.C. to window*) touched by magic. (*Door slowly opens, and a very beautiful but very prim girl* [*the Good Fairy*] *appears at door, and crosses U.L.C.*)

GOOD FAIRY. (*To Desmond*) You rang, sir?

WICKED FAIRY. (*U.C., horrified*) You? Here?

DESMOND (*Turns*) Who the devil are you?

GOOD FAIRY. Private Donovan. Your new driver, sir. Reporting for duty.

DESMOND. (*Rises, brushes dust off his knees*) I told you they'd come if I rang. But look here, what's happened to Private Nash?

GOOD FAIRY. Went sick, sir.

WICKED FAIRY. (*Takes a step toward Good Fairy, then crosses U.C. to window. Violent*) Why did you come here? Just as I was getting on so well!

DESMOND. (*Points to Wicked Fairy*) Donovan. D'you know this man?

GOOD FAIRY. (*Sadly*) Yes, sir.

DESMOND. Who is he?

GOOD FAIRY. I've known him for years, sir.

DESMOND. Eh? Where?

GOOD FAIRY. Everywhere.

DESMOND. For years? How many years?

GOOD FAIRY. About four thousand.

DESMOND. Donovan, I warn you, I'm in no mood for jollity.

GOOD FAIRY. I'm telling the truth, sir. I've brought the car.

DESMOND. What for?

GOOD FAIRY. To drive you to the castle.

DESMOND. I didn't order it.

GOOD FAIRY. You were going to, though, sir.

DESMOND. But you haven't answered my first question yet. Who is this fellow?

GOOD FAIRY. He's an old enemy. (*Fresh thought*) You'll have plenty of time to find out, sir, at the castle. (*Desmond crosses U.L., looks out door*)

WICKED FAIRY. (*Annoyed*) Are you coming, too?

THE LOVE OF FOUR COLONELS

GOOD FAIRY. I'm driving you.

WICKED FAIRY. There goes my fun. (*Sits chair L. of C. table*)

GOOD FAIRY. (*Seeing Ikonenko, who is still in a state of collapse. Crosses, leans over him*) Oh, the poor Colonel! (*Administering smelling salts, which she gets from her pocket*)

DESMOND. (*Crossing D.L.C.*) Donovan, will you kindly put the Colonel down, and inform me first of all about yourself, and then about this man.

GOOD FAIRY. (*Turns to him, smiles*) How are your dogs, sir—Ranger, Thunderbolt, and Black Havoc?

DESMOND. Extremely fit, thank you, by the latest reports. How do you know about them? (*Crosses below chair L.C.*)

GOOD FAIRY. Ah, Colonel Breitenspiegel, you were wrong to trust your wife's psychiatrist.

WESLEY. (*Standing U.R. corner of conference table*) Why?

GOOD FAIRY. He's been taking advantage of your absence. He took your wife to the Stork Club last night, and then—

WESLEY. What!

WICKED FAIRY. Spoilsport!

GOOD FAIRY. And you, Colonel Frappot. It was sinful of you to tell the Mayor that your wife was living with a transport chief while you are living with an actress. It's true that you live with an actress, but your wife is utterly faithful to this day, and lives in hopes.

AIMÉ. (*Unsurprised*) One tells little lies to appease one's conscience—and then, my wife's fidelity has always seemed to me so embarrassingly un-French.

GOOD FAIRY. Or just embarrassing?

AIMÉ. Or just embarrassing.

IKONENKO. (*Stirs, groans*) Where am I?

DESMOND. (*Crosses above sofa L.*) Steady, old man.

GOOD FAIRY. (*Going to him*) You've been a bad boy, Colonel Ikonenko, shooting at a man.

WICKED FAIRY. (*Cheery*) I forgive him!

IKONENKO. (*Writhing*) I have failed! I have failed!

GOOD FAIRY. No, my dear Colonel, you have not.

IKONENKO. My life is finished. I must go to Moscow and confess.

GOOD FAIRY. Oh, nonsense! You're coming to the castle with us.

IKONENKO. The castle . . . ?

GOOD FAIRY. Yes, to visit the Sleeping Beauty.

DESMOND. What's that?

GOOD FAIRY. Yes, sir, it's the castle where the Sleeping Beauty has been asleep for a hundred years.

DESMOND. Donovan, I warn you, I'm sure you're an excellent driver, but I won't have romancing.

AIMÉ. La Belle du Bois Dormant.

DESMOND. What?

AIMÉ. The Beauty of the Sleeping Forest. But then, who are you, Miss Donovan? (*Good Fairy looks around for a moment, in a quandary*)

WICKED FAIRY. (*Hurt*) Might as well tell them now. The harm's done. Thanks to you, you wily immortal bitch.

GOOD FAIRY. (*Smiles radiantly*) In the visible world, I have many names. In prehistory, I was the angel charged with the painful duty of chasing Adam and Eve out of the Garden of Eden. (*Racked with remorse*) Oh, if only I had been there first, I could have warned them . . .

WICKED FAIRY. (*Mocking*) But you weren't.

GOOD FAIRY. (*Sad*) I wasn't. And in the world of dreams and legends, they call me the Good Fairy.

AIMÉ. (*Softly*) And what do we call you?

GOOD FAIRY. (*With a shrug and a charming smile*) Donovan.

WICKED FAIRY. (*Piqued*) Well . . . is nobody going to ask me who *I* am?

DESMOND. We have done so consistently, sir. I can only take it as a reflection on your character that you have to be provoked into a confession by Donovan's good example. (*Aside*) Full marks, Donovan.

WICKED FAIRY. (*Scoffing*) Good example, my magic wand! (*Rises, crosses below table to R.*) In prehistory, I won my first victory over Donovan, in that same Garden of Eden where she first learned what she was up against. Yes. (*Turns vindictive*) I was the Serpent who gave Eve the forbidden apple. The Devil was absent. He didn't realize the importance of the occasion.

(Crosses U. to behind C. table) Since then, Donovan and I have been struggling for the driving-reins of this ramshackle carriage they call humanity—I can tempt, and so can Donovan, and you, gentlemen, are our battleground. You and Eve and the Sleeping Beauty, and all the peoples and dreams of the world. *(Picks up cloak and scarf, puts on latter. Suddenly agonized)* And you have the wonderful possibility of choosing . . . *(Puts on cloak, picks up hat)*

AIMÉ. Choosing? Why do you think that should give us so much pleasure? —But you did not tell, mon serpent—what is your name in that sweeter world?

WICKED FAIRY. Me? *(A peal of laughter, followed by an elaborate gesture)* Silly boy, I'm the Wicked Fairy! *(Lights dim out)*

Blackout

ACT ONE

Scene 2

Forest. All is dark. The only thing we can hear is a sound which may be music, of a deep, mysterious, and atmospheric sort.

WESLEY'S VOICE. (*Off R.*) Come on in here. (*Wesley enters R.*)

AIMÉ'S VOICE. (*Off R.*) Ow! (*Aimé enters R.*)

DESMOND'S VOICE. (*Off R.*) What is it? Oh, drat! (*Desmond enters R.*)

IKONENKO'S VOICE. (*Off R.*) A step, two steps, ai! (*Ikonenko enters R.*)

WESLEY. (*Carrying flashlight. Overawed*) Can you see anything? (*As the Colonels file in, he shines flashlight on the set, which reveals nothing but a forbidding screen of sagging gauzes*) Kind of eerie.

DESMOND. (*Behind Wesley, R.C.*) Can we have some light?

WICKED FAIRY. (*Crosses below group to C.*) How do you expect me to produce light?

DESMOND. Magic.

WICKED FAIRY. So you do admit of such a thing?

DESMOND. I'm not one to look a gift horse in the mouth. (*Front of stage becomes lighter*)

IKONENKO. (*Over L.C., eyes gleaming*) This might be the kind of castle where jewels lie hidden.

AIMÉ. Do I hear the people's representative hoping to find jewels?

WICKED FAIRY. The people's representative stole a diamond-studded watch from a German duchess.

IKONENKO. It's a lie. I exchanged it against a Soviet cuckoo-clock.

AIMÉ. Where will you take us from here?

WICKED FAIRY. (*Crosses D.C., turns to them, back to audience*) You're boys at heart, the four of you. You'd much rather explore than be shown anything, wouldn't you?

WESLEY. Sure. Speaking for myself.

WICKED FAIRY. (*Crosses U.C.*) Go on, then. I'll show you all you want to know, when you have found nothing. (*Aimé and Wesley exit L.*)

DESMOND. (*Crosses L., turns*) Where are you going to be? You won't leave us here alone?

WICKED FAIRY. We won't. I just want a word with Donovan.

DESMOND. Have I your word?

GOOD FAIRY. (*Entering R.*) You have my word.

DESMOND. Good enough for us, Donovan. (*Goes out L.*)

IKONENKO. I shall try the floorboards. (*Goes out L.*)

GOOD FAIRY. (*Crosses R.C. as Wicked Fairy looks off L.*) You want a word with me? Why?

WICKED FAIRY. I hardly know where to begin. That's odd for me, isn't it?

GOOD FAIRY. Are you trying to be sincere?

WICKED FAIRY. (*Looking away from her*) Isn't it embarrassing? (*Pause*) You see, in a strange way, these four idiots have touched me . . .

GOOD FAIRY. What game are you playing now?

WICKED FAIRY. My dear child, if I were playing a game, I'd do it in the usual way. I'm too old, too hidebound, for innovations. (*Softer*) I mean what I say with all the very limited sincerity at my disposal.

GOOD FAIRY. Why should these four have touched you, when you have ridden roughshod over the dead, and, even worse, the dying? When throughout our immortality you have spent your sleepless existence gloating over misery and vice?

WICKED FAIRY. (*Crossing in to C.*) That's just it. I'm beginning to tire. (*Pause*) Oh, Donovan, if you knew, if you could guess . . .

GOOD FAIRY. What?

WICKED FAIRY. How I am longing to do a good deed!

GOOD FAIRY. Ssh! (*Nervous*) Be careful what you say . . .

WICKED FAIRY. (*Turns L. and back*) I've become quite reckless. I sometimes can't bear to do the obvious. To maneuver happy wives into beds with uncongenial lovers—to send laughing little children onto railway tracks. It's all so easy. I'm such an expert in evil that there's no challenge any more. I dream of new worlds to conquer. I dream of one day saving a life . . . or at least of upholding a fidelity. Can you understand?

GOOD FAIRY. Too well! If you knew how the mawkishness of inhuman kindness had begun to bore me! Perfection is a stagnant thing. Oh, Serpent, I'm longing to be bad. Just for once.

WICKED FAIRY. Now I could almost forget who I am, and fall in love.

GOOD FAIRY. With me? Surely not.

WICKED FAIRY. Yes. One kiss would bring me peace for centuries. I could drain a little goodness from your lips, and it would linger through the years, tingeing the mind with sweetness, and making a memory of that empty space I call my heart.

GOOD FAIRY. And I could sense the poison of your tongue. I would be stung by the sadness of the world, and drown for a moment in the savage pallor of your eyes. Then I would taste of that bitter thing they call reality. (*They are standing close to each other. They move closer to each other. Wicked Fairy leans his head near her, his arms near her waist. Crash of thunder. Wicked Fairy goes R., reeling as if sent by an unknown force*) Oh, Serpent, dare we? (*Pause*) It was a silly game to have played. How I envy mortals.

WICKED FAIRY. They can choose between us. We have no choice.

GOOD FAIRY. No.

WICKED FAIRY. Donovan . . .

GOOD FAIRY. Mmm?

WICKED FAIRY. When we show them the Beauty, would we be failing in our duty if we agreed not to interfere for once?

GOOD FAIRY. (*Crossing R. to him*) You mean, if we let them try to awaken her love, each in his own way, without our influence?

WICKED FAIRY. Yes.

GOOD FAIRY. Is that possible? What could men do without good and evil? They too would lose the possibility of choice, the joy of strategy.

WICKED FAIRY. But love is stronger than choice. After all, it has even affected both of us . . . you the conscience, I the primitive desire.

GOOD FAIRY. (*Stepping back*) But can we trust ourselves not to interfere?

WICKED FAIRY. You mean, can you trust me?

GOOD FAIRY. (*Shy*) Yes . . .

WICKED FAIRY. I'll try to behave. I can't say more than that.

GOOD FAIRY. (*Tender*) No, you can't . . . (*Makes an instinctive movement toward him, but breaks away. The four Colonels are heard. They enter R.*)

WESLEY. (*As Ikonenko crosses D.L.*) This place is like a maze.

AIMÉ. (*Crossing R. in front of Wesley*) Of what period is the architecture?

WICKED FAIRY. (*Abstracted, gazing tenderly at Good Fairy*) Modern . . .

AIMÉ. What?

WICKED FAIRY. (*Recovering, as Good Fairy steps L.*) Oh, (*Turns*) I beg your pardon. Comparatively modern: thirteenth-century. It was built by Otho, First Grand Duke of Burg zu Burg-Burg von Herzogenburg. A charming man.

GOOD FAIRY. A brute.

WICKED FAIRY. His successor, Willibald, was a relatively weedy boy of seven foot two, who was a perfect pest.

GOOD FAIRY. Or, no, he relieved me of a great deal of worry.

WICKED FAIRY. He was the first man to fit a primitive equivalent of a Yale lock onto a chastity belt.

IKONENKO. May we visit some of the rooms?

WICKED FAIRY. You will do better. You will see the Sleeping Beauty. She will wake up soon.

AIMÉ. But the legend says she will wake only when Prince Charming kisses her, at the end of a hundred years.

WICKED FAIRY. This will be a temporary awakening for your benefit. She will have to sleep again later. That is—unless *you* succeed.

IKONENKO. Succeed? —Succeed at what?

WICKED FAIRY. In making your ideal a reality, by seducing her.

WESLEY. (*Crossing to Wicked Fairy*) What are we waiting for? Is she yummy?

WICKED FAIRY. Is she what?

WESLEY. Has she got *it*?

WICKED FAIRY. What?

DESMOND. Is she personable?

AIMÉ. Est-ce-qu'elle a du chien?

THE LOVE OF FOUR COLONELS

WICKED FAIRY. Du chien?

IKONENKO. Is she sexually attractive?

DESMOND. (*A step D.R.*) Really! He's damned coarse, this fellow.

WICKED FAIRY. Now, stand over there, if you please. Donovan! (*Turns, facing U., raises arms*) I must ask for complete silence. (*Desmond crosses L.*)

ACT ONE

Scene 3

The two Fairies stand down C. with their backs to audience, and raise their arms. As they do so, the stage grows dark, to notes of glacial music. When the lights come up again, they reveal the proscenium of a court theater of the early nineteenth century. It is elaborate and golden, with all the attendant symbolism of this type of erection. Two small royal boxes L. In them the King and Queen asleep. In U.L. box, King leans drunkenly over parapet. Queen lies back, sleeping and aghast. In box on R. (lower box, upper one is empty), Chamberlain sits ossified. On the stage, a fantastic and elaborate bed, in which lies the veiled and fragile figure of the Sleeping Beauty. Music stops. Wicked Fairy is now D.R., Good Fairy is U.R. Ikonenko crosses D.L.

IKONENKO. (*Suddenly filled with wonder, standing below box L.*) It is exactly as I have always imagined it.

AIMÉ. No, it is as I have often seen it in illustrations, and therefore not as I had imagined it. The French genius is the genius of mistrust.

DESMOND. (*At box L. between Aimé and Ikonenko*) Plenty of time for philosophizing later. (*Crosses C.*) Donovan, put me in the picture. (*Wicked Fairy takes off cloak and scarf, puts them on rail of box R., then moves U. onto step, and to R. corner*)

GOOD FAIRY. Yes, sir. We are in the court theater of King Florestan the Twenty-fourth, which was added to the castle in 1816. In spite of the Queen, whom you see sleeping up there, he had a . . . a morganatic arrangement with an actress. (*All the*

52

THE LOVE OF FOUR COLONELS

men step toward C., turn and look U. to box opposite) It happened a hundred years ago today. It was Aurora's birthday, and I was among the guests. My friend here, Carabosse—

DESMOND. Who?

WICKED FAIRY. Me. Carabosse. Not my real name. A kind of nom-de-fée.

DESMOND. I see. Go on, Donovan.

GOOD FAIRY. Carabosse was, for obvious reasons, not in the King's engagement book, and he was not invited to the christening—

IKONENKO. But every child knows this story!

DESMOND. (*Turns, then turns back*) Every child may, but there are still a few colonels who do not. Go on, Donovan.

GOOD FAIRY. Carabosse, who is very spiteful, was determined to be revenged, and therefore uttered a terrible curse on this house.

WESLEY. What do you know!

GOOD FAIRY. The curse was that should Aurora ever prick herself with anything sharp, she would die. Naturally, we kept everything remotely sharp away from her. It worked, until this terrible day. (*Self-effacing*) In my infinite innocence—

WICKED FAIRY. (*With a cackle*) Bravo!

GOOD FAIRY. In my infinite innocence, I wrote a play, a pastoral piece in rhyming couplets.

WICKED FAIRY. Sickly as a piece of Turkish Delight.

GOOD FAIRY. In it I foolishly placed a spinning wheel. However, the needle was made of twisted silver paper, and could not hurt a fly. (*Remorseful*) I was not to know that the chamberlain, who is now asleep in the box—(*A step R., indicating him*) I was not to know that he was unreliable.

WICKED FAIRY. Unreliable! The most reliable man I ever employed.

GOOD FAIRY. Exactly. (*Turns, crosses C.*) He was charged with the stage management, and he substituted a real needle for the paper one. Aurora pricked herself with it in the third act, when the entire court was charmed by her exquisite purity. She died. I brought her back to life, but she fell into a deep sleep, and there she lies . . .

WICKED FAIRY. (*Crosses down to R.*) The rest is up to you.

WESLEY. What can we do?

WICKED FAIRY. Win her heart. Tempt her, as I tempted Eve—only, I warn you, your task will be more difficult, as she is not yet married. (*Crosses to Good Fairy*) May they go and look at her, do you think?

GOOD FAIRY. (*To Wicked Fairy: schoolmasters discussing the future of the boys—crossing below Wicked Fairy to D.R.*) I see no harm in it, so long as they don't touch her.

WICKED FAIRY. No, they mustn't touch her. (*To Colonels*) All right, go and look at her, but don't touch her. (*The four Colonels clamber onto stage. Desmond follows Wesley, crossing R. on stage. Takes off hat. Wesley goes U.R. of bed. Desmond is D.R., two steps away. Aimé goes U.L., then comes down L of bed. Ikonenko remains U.L.*)

GOOD FAIRY. What shall we do next?

THE LOVE OF FOUR COLONELS

WICKED FAIRY. (*Cruelly, as he steps down to her, and Ikonenko crosses to D.L. of bed, then to U.L.*) Why do you ask me?

GOOD FAIRY. Evil always has the initiative.

WICKED FAIRY. I'll tell you exactly what we will do—we will continue with the theatrical performance now after an interval of a hundred years. We will give a performance couched deeply in the Colonels' imagination. (*He is R.C.*)

GOOD FAIRY. I don't understand.

WICKED FAIRY. (*U.R.C.*) Look at them up there, prowling round her like wolves round the sheeps' pen. To them she is the ideal. They all see her in different ways. Only lust is common to them all.

GOOD FAIRY. (*Suffering—turns away to R.*) Yes.

WICKED FAIRY. When we bring Aurora back to momentary life, let's see whether men are as angelic as you think you have made them, or whether they are the cesspits I know them to be. (*Moves away to R.C.*)

GOOD FAIRY. (*Taking a step L. to him*) Carabosse, I warn you, if you try to help men to rape their ideals, to destroy what is sacred and untouchable in their natures, I shall protect the Beauty with all my strength.

WICKED FAIRY. (*Casual, and a little hurt*) I give my promise.

GOOD FAIRY. Without interference?

WICKED FAIRY. Without interference.

GOOD FAIRY. All right.

WESLEY. (*Turns away to R., calls from upper stage*) Hey, Fairies, I'm in love!

WICKED FAIRY. What did I tell you? (*Crosses to L. box*)

DESMOND. She's damned attractive. A lovely, fair-haired English rose.

WESLEY. (*Down toward Desmond*) Fair? She's got red hair, like flame.

AIMÉ. (*Down R., steps back to audience*) Red? She's the type of dark Mediterranean beauty one finds in Marseilles.

IKONENKO. (*Crossing L.*) Dark? A typical distortion. She is flaxen, like the farm girls in the Ukraine. Her face betrays deep convictions and a desire for immediate motherhood.

WICKED FAIRY. (*At L. box*) You're all in love with her?

WESLEY. (*With boundless enthusiasm*) Sure!

DESMOND. I must say she strikes a chord in me that has not been struck since my cadet days.

AIMÉ. (*Goes diagonally L., crossing Ikonenko*) I don't know whether I have the capacity for a love which is free from the selfish maneuvers of a carnal attachment. However, I am not a fool. I would like to sleep with her.

IKONENKO. (*Crossing C.*) I have already made my position clear in this matter.

WICKED FAIRY. Very well, gentlemen, we shall wake her up. But first we will wake up the chamberlain. (*Crosses to Good Fairy, R.*)

GOOD FAIRY. (*As she crosses U.R.C. to meet him—urgently*) Why?

WICKED FAIRY. To work the curtain. He's the stage manager—

have you forgotten? (*To Good Fairy*) Have I your permission to proceed?

GOOD FAIRY. Slowly, so I can see what you are doing. (*A step U.R.*)

WICKED FAIRY. (*Crossing to box*)
    Chamberlain! Awake, awake,
    For sin's sweet sake!
(*Chamberlain wakes noisily. A repellent old individual dressed in clothes of 1850, halfway between a footman and an undertaker*)

CHAMBERLAIN. Carabosse! The needle. It worked. (*Laughs hideously*)

WICKED FAIRY. (*Impatiently*) A hundred years have passed since then.

CHAMBERLAIN. Eh? What? I must have dozed off during the performance. Bad play. Thoroughly bad play.

WICKED FAIRY. (*Brutal*) Back to the wings. At once!

CHAMBERLAIN. (*Getting out of box. Crosses C. to U.L.*) Oh, dear! Oh, dear!

WICKED FAIRY. Back to work the curtain!

CHAMBERLAIN. Oh, dear . . . (*Goes toward stage, mumbling. Goes U.L., steps on platform, and exits L., just behind boxes*)

DESMOND. That must be the Mayor's great-grandfather.

WICKED FAIRY. Ring the curtain down. (*Goes U.C., beckons Colonels to gather about him. He is very secretive. Good Fairy crosses to upstage side of box. Desmond moves C.*) A word in your ear about—(*Wicked Fairy points to Beauty. He appears*

58   THE LOVE OF FOUR COLONELS

about to impart a confidence to Colonels, who cluster around him in C. of stage, by footlights. Suddenly the curtain-within-a-curtain falls, leaving Colonels outside. Wicked Fairy cackles. Colonels are caught unawares, and are annoyed)

WESLEY. Hey, what's happened to the girl?

WICKED FAIRY. (*D.C.*) You shall see her, if you are good. (*Colonels come, L. steps, down from stage to box L. on forestage*)

AIMÉ. (*Crosses L., off inner stage, then to L. to Wicked Fairy*) What do you wish us to do? (*Ikonenko crosses D.L.*)

WICKED FAIRY. Be the character you always hoped to be in your child's heart.

AIMÉ. I have no illusions. The character I always hoped to be is myself.

WICKED FAIRY. Have you no favorite period in history?

AIMÉ. Ah, yes. That is different. The turn of the eighteenth century, when France was inundated with the sun, reflected off her sovereign's pride.

WICKED FAIRY. Will you go first?

AIMÉ. Where to?

WICKED FAIRY. To act your love to your ideal.

AIMÉ. (*Falters*) Here?

WICKED FAIRY. Up on the stage! Now! Go into the wings—you will find all there to fit your most private dreams.

AIMÉ. And she will appear—

THE LOVE OF FOUR COLONELS

WICKED FAIRY. —As your ideal. As your hope. As what you left behind when you first knew a woman! (*Aimé takes step L., then back to Wicked Fairy*)

AIMÉ. One moment. Who *is* the Beauty?

WICKED FAIRY. I have told you. Your ideal. The ideal of all your sex.

AIMÉ. I am not prepared to share my ideal with everyone.

WICKED FAIRY. (*Turns R., then back*) Damned French pride. She is what you see in her, and what you see in her is your own cherished vision. (*After a moment of hesitation, Aimé runs off into wings, L. Wicked Fairy crosses U.R. to C. of platform, calls into orchestra pit*) Music! Herr Doktor Gimpel, Herr Doktor Straubel, Herr Professor Kampff: "Awake, awake, for sin's sweet sake." (*The three instruments begin tuning up*) Music of the eighteenth century, please! Hey presto, hey lento, hey allegro—ma non troppo!

DESMOND. (*A step to L.C.*) I say, what *is* going on? Are we to be treated to a theatrical performance? And if so, why?

WICKED FAIRY. It will be your turn next.

DESMOND. Mine?

WICKED FAIRY. (*Crossing R. on stage*) Yes. You too will become upon the stage your secret self, in quest of your ideal. Now sit down.

DESMOND. Where?

WICKED FAIRY. (*As music starts*) There. (*Indicates one of boxes at L. of stage. Desmond crosses to box at L. Sits in chair C. Wesley crosses into box, sits in U. chair. Ikonenko crosses to* box, sits in D. chair) We will sit here. (*Crosses R. and D. on forestage R. Indicates box on R. side.*)

GOOD FAIRY. (*Enters R. box quickly, goes to U. seat*) How kind of you to offer me a chair.

WICKED FAIRY. (*Getting into box R., puts cloak down on C. chair*) So much of my time is spent with the upper classes. (*Good Fairy and Wicked Fairy sit, Wicked Fairy on D. chair*)

IKONENKO. I don't understand what this performance will prove. (*During this last speech lights in the boxes and forestage slowly dim out, leaving us in semidarkness except for the glow of the few footlights which the Chamberlain will have time to light. All is silence and expectancy—except for the distant scratching of the orchestra—when, to our surprise, the house lights begin to creep up and the curtain comes slowly down*)

WICKED FAIRY. (*Rises*) Prove! You are in the theater, after all, gentlemen. Now may I crave your silence while we see the naked soul of a certain Colonel Aimé Frappot chasing the shadow of the elusive bird which flutters in his heart. And, may he catch it! (*Sits in box*)

CURTAIN

ACT TWO

FRENCH SCENE

photo by Fred Fehl

ACT TWO

As curtain rises the stage is exactly as we last saw it. Chamberlain is just about to light the last remaining footlights, and as he exits R. the curtain-within-a-curtain rises, revealing the Beauty sitting at her dressing table, with her hand mirror.

DESMOND. (*In L. box, sitting in C. chair*) Who's that?

GOOD FAIRY. (*Sitting in U.C. chair, R. box—enchanted*) The Beauty. How lovely she looks in that costume!

IKONENKO. (*Loud*) That's not the Beauty!

WICKED FAIRY. (*In R. box*) Of course it is, idiot! Aimé's Beauty. He chose the eighteenth century.

BEAUTY. (*Puts down hand mirror as music stops*) Heigh-ho! It is but eleven o'clock in the morning, and already I am awake, for when a woman of the town must choose a husband, it is wise to rise early.

IKONENKO. Eleven o'clock is late, not early.

WICKED FAIRY. Sssh! Give your colleague a chance.

BEAUTY. Husband! What a tedious thing is man when he is called by the vile name of husband! —And yet (*Rises, crosses D.C.*) were there no husband, the little lapses that women of the town dote upon would lack of savor. (*Laughs*) Yes, I have ribboned bonnets, a wardrobe as fine as the richest in Paris, periwigs and toys and baubles, pretty little dogs, black boys to serve the chocolate, a Dutch milliner, an Italian dancing master, and all that elegance could wish. (*Melancholy*) Yet now I lack a lover. But first, a husband, for without a husband to deceive, a lover's an empty pleasure. (*Crosses U.C. Doorbell rings*) But hist, one comes! (*Sits L.*) I shall dissemble. (*Aimé enters, immensely romantic in the costume of the period*)

AIMÉ. (*Bowing deeply, C.*) Mademoiselle, methought this to be a coffee-house.

BEAUTY. A coffee-house, sir? A coffee-house, sir? How came you by this notion?

AIMÉ. I know not, and it matters less. (*Aside*) I had observed her through the window while in quest of a coffee-house. My taste for coffee was dispersed.

BEAUTY. (*Aside*) A bold gallant, too good for husbanding. I shall pretend to hate him. (*Crossing to Aimé*) Sir, that you were in search of a coffee-house, I doubt not. That you have found one, however, I doubt much. I pray you turn about and *find* a coffee-house. (*Wicked Fairy exits unseen from box R.*)

AIMÉ. (*Aside*) Which means she loves me. (*To her*) If I were sure, Mademoiselle, that the coffee-house would hold such charms as these, still I would not go, for what fool would inspire your respect and not stay to enjoy it?

BEAUTY. (*Aside*) I doubt that it is my respect he wants. Yes, alas, he is too good for husband, and too soon for lover! (*Aimé kneels, kisses her hand, stands again.* —*To him*) Are you not afraid to incur my wrath, sir?

AIMÉ. No, Mademoiselle, for it is a la mode to hate in public those you would tumble in private. (*Hand on her waist*)

BEAUTY. (*Crossing below him to D.R.—aside*) He speaks like a

THE LOVE OF FOUR COLONELS

gentleman, indeed. (*Crosses to him*) Then I, sir, am not of the rule, for when I hate, I hate, and there's an end to't.

AIMÉ. (*Aside*) She loves me more with every phrase she utters. (*To her*) Then, Madam, I am here to a double purpose.

BEAUTY. Nay, nay, why do you call me "Madam" now?

AIMÉ. You have a short wind for raillery, Madam, which betokens that you are but lately brought to bed by a husband, and have not yet wearied of his palsied face upon your pillow.

BEAUTY. (*Crosses D.R.—aside*) Now I could love him, indeed. Were't better to admit I am a maid, or, sighing, say, "Alas, sir, what you suppose is true. I have a husband."

AIMÉ. (*Aside*) See, she sighs and moans, and each heaving of those twin rotundities doth seem to beckon me.

BEAUTY. (*Crossing to him*) Sir, I am indeed cursed with a husband, as hideous a vaporous wretch as was ever purged by physic, for indeed all he touches, or breathes upon—or fondles—has upon it the cloying stench of pharmacy.

AIMÉ. Ha!

BEAUTY. (*Aside*) I have affected him.

AIMÉ. (*Aside*) I will approach her. (*Circles box, crossing R. behind her, and around in front to his original position*)

BEAUTY. (*Aside*) Heigh-ho, how sweet is the lot of woman when it is not miserable. (*To him*) Have you done prowling, **sir?**

AIMÉ. (*L., aside*) So? She is impatient?

BEAUTY. (*Aside*) This then is the calm which, preceding the storm, doth make the storm so very much more enjoyable.

(*Crosses to C. of settee. Sits, beckons him with her finger. Aimé moves in and kneels*) I shall scream, sir!

AIMÉ. Untruss, ma'am, untruss!

BEAUTY. I shall box your ears, sir.

AIMÉ. (*His hands on her waist, he forces her to rise*) You conspire to add to their delight!

BEAUTY. (*Rising, going to R. of settee, and behind it*) I shall black your eye, sir!

AIMÉ. (*As Beauty comes around L. end of settee and Aimé follows*) And surround your image with a coronet of stars!

BEAUTY. I shall smack your cheek, sir!

AIMÉ. (*Taking her in his arms*) To aid a lover's blush!

BEAUTY. (*Pummeling him*) I shall pummel you, sir!

AIMÉ. (*Still holding her in his arms*) And I shall think it is the beating of your heart!

BEAUTY. Help, help! (*As he has almost stolen the fatal kiss*) I am a virgin, sir!

DESMOND. (*Rises, then sits*) Good God!

AIMÉ. (*Releasing her abruptly*) How? How's this? (*The other Colonels relax, go back to their seats*)

BEAUTY. (*Pouting*) I lied . . . a little lie, sir, to fan the flame of ardor. (*Sits on sofa*)

AIMÉ. (*With aloof savagery*) You call it a little lie, Miss, to create (*Moving back of sofa*) a husband i' the mind as full of good solid, husbandly vices as the million others of the cursed band? (*L. of sofa*) You call it a little lie to drive me on in the hope of theft, to find that you are ownerless? You call it a little lie to flatter me by breathing scandal of an imaginary spouse? L'impertinence de cet enfant!

BEAUTY. (*Rises—aside, crossing L. to face wall*) How he glowers! I must appease him, for he is a handsome enough coxcomb, and may have his uses. I will sing awhile. (*Aloud—crosses L., dancing*) La-la-la. Fol-de-rol-lol.

GOOD FAIRY. Oh, thank goodness.

IKONENKO. (*Exploding*) That's not the Beauty! Where are her motherly virtues? (*Beauty touches his shoulder, then crosses R. to settee, sits*)

DESMOND. I certainly can't call this lass innocent. Is that what he sees in her?

WESLEY. She sure knows her way around.

GOOD FAIRY. (*Sighs*) Yes, that's what he sees in her. But the fatal kiss was avoided—that's all I care about.

DESMOND. (*Rising*) But, Donovan, are you *sure* it's the same girl as I saw sleeping up there? Admittedly, there's a superficial resemblance, but—

GOOD FAIRY. It's the same girl, sir. You will see her in a different light when your turn comes.

IKONENKO. (*As Desmond sits*) Have they finished? Has he failed?

GOOD FAIRY. Yes—Carabosse. (*Suddenly jumps up*) Where is he?

DESMOND. Who?

GOOD FAIRY. Carabosse!

DESMOND. He's gone! (*Not at all. He enters the stage C., as the very description which the Beauty gave of her imaginary husband*)

WICKED FAIRY. (*Entering U.C., goes to behind sofa*) So soon abroad, my love, my chick, my doll? And hast thou drunk thy chocolate yet, and hast thou learned thy minuet and little songs, and hast thou pretty things to tell me? Hm? Eh?

GOOD FAIRY. (*Heart cry*) I knew he'd have to interfere!

WICKED FAIRY. (*Crossing D.R. corner of upper stage—aside to Good Fairy*) My nature was too strong for me! If he keeps on doing this—he'll never get around to doing that. (*Moves U. to sofa*)

GOOD FAIRY. You haven't beaten me yet! (*Runs off R.*)

AIMÉ. (*Over to L.*) Oons! It is her father!

WICKED FAIRY. (*D.R.*) Zounds! I am her husband!

BEAUTY. (*Rising*) My husband, say you?

AIMÉ. How? (*Aside*) Thus was her lie no lie at all, but a strategy to draw out my anguish, and with my anguish, my delight!

BEAUTY. (*Aside*) That I have no husband I am sure, though I'm eager to acquire one. This old fool is ugly enough—and blind enough, for if he mistake me for his wife now he will again, or I'll see to't. (*Steps back to L. of settee*)

WICKED FAIRY. (*Using lorgnette*) Madam, I pray you, tell me who is this gallant who appears to be studying the wall with such grave and scholarly attention?

BEAUTY (*With deep disdain*) That is my eunuch, sir. (*Aimé turns and looks at her*)

WICKED FAIRY. An eunuch, Madam?

BEAUTY. Yes, an eunuch from the Ottoman realm.

WICKED FAIRY. (*Aside*) Yeah, straight from the ottoman, I'll warrant. Her hair is all unkempt, while he doth avert his eyes to cover his confusion. I'll talk with him. (*Aloud*) Sir! (*Crosses C. to L.*) Sir, I say!

AIMÉ. (*Falsetto—turns to Wicked Fairy*) Sir, I am your honor's most obliged, most devoted servant.

WICKED FAIRY. (*Aside*) There's truth in't, then. (*Aloud*) And I yours, sir, I assure you. (*Aimé makes low bow. Beauty pretends to faint*)

BEAUTY. Oh! I faint! Help! (*Drops onto settee, head at R. end. Aimé throws her a kiss.*)

WICKED FAIRY. My knicknack! My bee! My grouse! My pigeon! My widgeon! What ails thee?

BEAUTY. A lack of breath, sir.

WICKED FAIRY. Which physic declares to be no more than an over-excess of vacuum.

BEAUTY. And a swimming of the brain, sir.

WICKED FAIRY. Yes, yes, an insufficiency of manual torpor.

BEAUTY. And a stopping of the heart, sir.

WICKED FAIRY. Or a lack of movement in the sentimental regions. (*Touches her breasts—she slaps his hand*) Attend me, my nightingale, my owlkin, my night-jar. I'll fetch thee medicine straight. Meanwhile, loosen your corsets. (*In pantomime urges Aimé to come over to the reclining Beauty, and exits R. Meantime Beauty rises, takes Aimé's hand, turns below him, to his L. Aimé and Beauty fly into each other's arms. They are about to kiss, when Good Fairy enters C., disguised. She crosses L.C.*)

GOOD FAIRY. Hold!

AIMÉ. (*Out of character, faltering*) Jeanette . . .

BEAUTY. (*Swings below him to his R.*) What name was that? (*Aimé releases her*) Thy wife?

AIMÉ. My mistress.

BEAUTY. (*Crossing C. to between them—curtsies*) How? Thou hast a mistress—and a wife? How have I been deceived! Nay, sir, I will not love thee, for to be one of an entire sex verges upon the indiscriminate, and with that I send thee packing, sir. (*Crosses U.C.*)

AIMÉ. (*Aside*) Ah, how a refusal should spur me on! And yet—

GOOD FAIRY. Come then, sir, content yourself with a well-remembered face. The lines of sorrow upon it are your own. (*Aimé smiles at her*) Canst see thy signature upon my cheeks, thy seal upon my lips? And canst see thy younger self reflected in my eyes?

AIMÉ. Thou art like an old song, but ill-remembered.

GOOD FAIRY. And quick to learn again? (*She holds out her hands to Aimé, and Beauty, seeing it, holds hers out. Aimé considers, crosses to Good Fairy, seizes her hands, kisses them. Beauty bursts into tears, sits. Wicked Fairy enters with bottle, crosses to settee*)

WICKED FAIRY. (*Crossing behind sofa to C.*) Here's medicine, my cake, my bun, my sweetmeat . . . (*He senses situation, loses all sense of character as well as his temper, and shouts, stamps his gouty foot, howls*) Oh, Donovan! Curtain! Bring it down! (*Consternation. Curtain falls*)

DESMOND. (*Rises, crosses from box L.C.*) What d'you make of it?

WESLEY. (*Sitting on edge of box L.*) I didn't understand his motivation.

IKONENKO. He treated her like a swine.

WESLEY. Why did he want her to be married?

DESMOND. He's always given me the impression of a fellow who's a bit sick of women, but who can't leave them alone.

WESLEY. Yeah, but that doesn't explain why he throws over a girl as fresh as that for the second dame.

DESMOND. Yes. She was a bit long in the tooth. What did he call her? Jeanette? The whole thing is very peculiar, if you ask me. (*A step D.L.C.*)

WICKED FAIRY. (*Looking through curtains of C. opening—curtains of inner stage*) Colonel Rinder-Sparrow.

DESMOND. (*Turns U.L.C.*) Eh?

WICKED FAIRY. How do you see yourself?

DESMOND. What?

WICKED FAIRY. What is the embodiment of your romantic self?

DESMOND. (*Turns away to L.*) Goodness knows.

WESLEY. You probably see yourself as a golden retriever.

DESMOND. No need to be rude about dogs, Wesley. They have finer souls than you or I.

WESLEY. O.K. Go up there as one. See the Beauty as a pekinese.

DESMOND. Just a minute. There was a bloke who always fascinated me.

WICKED FAIRY. Who?

DESMOND. When I was small, and allowed to stay up late with the grownups, there was a family portrait just opposite my chair, and while my parents were talking about this and that, I used to stare and stare . . .

WICKED FAIRY. Who was it?

DESMOND. The first of the Rinders. My mother's a Sparrow, you see. He was the private secretary to Lord Burghley's personal choirmaster, and died of a cholic condition in the spring of 1616. He had the most extraordinary—

WICKED FAIRY. (*Very bored, yawns*) Colonel, will you come onto the stage, please?

DESMOND. (*Crossing U.L., starts to exit L.*) Wish me luck.

WESLEY. Oh, no. I'll wish myself that.

DESMOND. That attitude, Wesley, won't get you anywhere. (*Goes into wings off L.*)

WICKED FAIRY. (*Calling into orchestra pit*) Orchestra! The music of England's Golden Age! (*Exits behind curtains. A pavane is started. Aimé enters L., back in uniform. He seems weary. Chamberlain enters, lights footlights during ensuing dialogue*)

WESLEY. Ah, Aimé. We've been discussing the motivations. (*Aimé comes down L. inner stage steps, going a little R.*)

AIMÉ. I failed. I knew I would.

WESLEY. But why in the hell did you insist that she was married?

AIMÉ. Does it not disgust you when men of our age cast their shadow over youth and blissful inexperience? I am a lover, Wesley, not a corrupter.

WESLEY. Do you mean you were being unselfish?

AIMÉ. It is a relief when selfishness and unselfishness come to the same thing. I do not enjoy seducing youth.

IKONENKO. But who is Jeanette?

AIMÉ. Jeanette? My mistress in Paris.

WESLEY. The actress?

AIMÉ. The actress. She is not beautiful, but she is sad, and I like sadness. She is also safe. We lost our illusions with our second kiss, and our third was more passionate than the first.

IKONENKO. Still, you made every effort to make love to the Beauty.

AIMÉ. (*Turning away, looks U. stage*) I wonder if I did.

IKONENKO. Your intentions were clear to the spectator. Clear and reprehensible.

AIMÉ. I saw Jeanette again with what was almost relief.

WESLEY. Tell me, as man to man, what do you see in Jeanette, physically?

GOOD FAIRY. (*Entering through R. box, crossing R.C.*) What does any man see in his conscience?

IKONENKO. (*Rising, crossing L.C.—to Aimé*) I fail to understand, Frappot, how you can have chosen as a favorite period the epoch of pre-revolutionary France.

AIMÉ. Why?

IKONENKO. The insincerities which led relentlessly to the Revolution were already painfully in evidence.

AIMÉ. (*Lively*) Insincerities? Mon Dieu, they said what they thought in those days, and said it wittily.

IKONENKO. Wit is unnecessary.

AIMÉ. So is life.

IKONENKO. No, my friend, you are wrong. Life is necessary, for without life the world would be unpopulated.

AIMÉ. And a great relief.

IKONENKO. That is an offensive remark.

GOOD FAIRY. I quite agree.

IKONENKO. Without population, there could be no working class. That is in itself sufficient reason for population.

GOOD FAIRY. And where does God take His place in your conception?

WICKED FAIRY. (*Looking through curtains*) No canvassing! The play begins. I hope this time with satisfactory results.

GOOD FAIRY. It depends on you. (*Good Fairy crosses R., sits box R. Ikonenko crosses back to his chair in box. Wicked Fairy exits R. Curtain rises on inner stage. Dim corridors of castle. Desmond is discovered, bearded, and dressed in elaborate Elizabethan costume. There is a property rock down C. Wesley sits on U.R. chair, Aimé on C. chair*)

DESMOND (*Standing C.*)
The day speeds sullenly to its decline
And yet all's unachieved.
Five gray eagles cackled at my birth
And the entrails of a wasp lay, by dint of magic,
At my moaning mother's feet, who, being brought to bed
Of a two-months' child, did presently faint,
And pine, and die, aweary of her sire's black reproaches,

(*Crosses D.C.*)
Which, being the first sounds to play upon this Desmond's ear,
Did fill full his thoughts with hatred of all chastity.

(*Beauty appears R. and crosses above Desmond to L. stage and off*)

IKONENKO. This is more like the Beauty. (*Beauty reaches L.C.*)

DESMOND. (*Follows Beauty, crossing L.C.*)
There lingers in the mind
A vision of such galling purity
That I must defile it quick, or call myself
No more Desmonio.

(*Moves C.*)
Twenty years ago by the light of the lately dwindling moon
Did I pit my passion against an Illyrian nun—

76   THE LOVE OF FOUR COLONELS

"My vows, my vows," she cried, but 'twas in vain—
A maidenhead well lost's a mistress' gain.

(*Trumpets. He crosses U.R. The Beauty re-enters sleepwalking, L. to R. below Desmond. She is fair, lovely, and desperately Elizabethan. Desmond crosses D.C. by rock, looks off R.*)
Now here's Aurora, betrothed to chastity,
I'll to her while her heart's enfeebled by her grief.
For when a man is bent on sin
His conscience does fly out, his lewdness in!
(*Starts L., pointing L. hand*)

WESLEY. (*Calls, points*) Hey! She went the other way! (*Desmond turns, goes R., exits R.*)

BEAUTY. (*Enters R., crosses to C.*)
Ah, could I but while away the restless hours
Enshrouded in oblivion! This woman's shape
A prison is. These hands, ten twigs, but petal-soft,
These arms, roads that lead into the air
From this all-too-solid dish of garnished bones
That men lust after. These breasts, that never will give suck,
This face, this outline of perfection, this sketch of beauty,
This mirror which, held up, reflects the nothingness within.
This belly, this empty cell, this resting-place
Of the unborn, forever uninhabited, an echoing vault,
These legs, these slender columns which bind me to the earth,
These restless travelers whose path runs wild
From the nowhere of birth to the nowhere of death
Through the nowhere in between.
(*Desmond enters U.R.*)
                                        I have grown
Weary of breathing. Patience, enfold me then,
And death, be kind.

DESMOND. (*Crossing D.C. to Beauty*)
  Death be kind,
  But life be kinder first.

BEAUTY. What's he that enters? Art thou a ghost?

DESMOND. (*Behind her*)
  Nay, Aurora, but a geography of rivers red
  Which break their banks and rush for thee
  In one cascading tide. Music, ho!
(*Music starts*)

BEAUTY. (*Crossing L.*)
  How dulcet is the virginal!

DESMOND. (*Crossing L.*)
  And dulcet thou, of all most virginal.

BEAUTY.
  Art thou a man? For if thou art
(*Crosses below him to R.*)
  Get thee to some more frolicsome abode,
  And do thy wenching there.

DESMOND. (*Crossing R.*)
  I shall stay here, and we will sink
  Our frantic hearts in a sweet sleep.
(*He seizes her, his arms encircle her shoulders*)

BEAUTY. (*Livid, throwing him off, turns to him, backs him to U.L.C.*)
  Thou toad-spawn, thine own second worser self,
  Thou yellow painted bauble,
  Thou wasp without a sting, thou yolkless egg,
  I'll none of thee. Go sing thy amorous odes to statues,
(*Desmond sits on rock*)
  Get with child a tree-stump. Marry a broomstick. Away!

DESMOND. (*Rises, crosses to her*)
   Nay. Then if I have thee not
   Let no man have thee!
(*He draws a knife. Attacks her as she dodges to L., circling twice around rock. Gets knife stuck in floor as she runs around. Pulls knife out. Catches Beauty C. and goes R. of her. Wicked Fairy enters as a clown. Good Fairy rises precipitately*)

WICKED FAIRY. Hold, sirrah!

GOOD FAIRY. He's done it again! (*She rushes out of box to R.*)

WICKED FAIRY. (*Hitting Desmond with bladder, gets on rock*)
   'Tis of no avail to stab a monument
   Upon which mournful pigeons sit,
   And spill their droppings, which do go for tears.

BEAUTY. (*L.*) Oh, foolish fool.

WICKED FAIRY. How should I not be foolish, being a fool, for were I not a fool, I would be wise, the less like thee, for thou, good lady, art in no wise wise (*Gets off rock*) and no wise foolish, and not foolish wise, and no wit either, for to be without wit is (*Sits on rock*) to be neither, therefore thou'rt in no wit wise and in no wise witty, and fall'st on thy bum 'twixt Grandam Nature's twin stools.

BEAUTY. (*A step D.L.*) I am in no humor for mirth, boy.

WICKED FAIRY. (*Crossing to her at L., imitating her*) I am in no humor for mirth, wench.

WESLEY. This must have amused the audiences of the time.

BEAUTY. I weep.

WICKED FAIRY. (*L.C.*) Nay, nay, an thou weeps't, thou art no monument. Thou art a fountain, lady. I shall be abroad, and weep myself, and say, "My lady is the breathing stuff of sprats, the nourishment of frogs, the comforter of dogs, (*Squats on floor*) for they do cock their legs at her as I do cock my snook." (*He pulls a long nose*)

BEAUTY.
My tears do turn to tears of laughter,
And I do hate thee for it.

DESMOND. (*Aside—crossing to her, over her shoulder*)
This boy doth serve my purpose well.

WICKED FAIRY. Hate me, madam, if it help thee know thyself, for I have as many names as I have faces, and if there's one of me you hate, there's ten more left to love.

BEAUTY. Thou sayest true, boy, and I do love thee well.

WICKED FAIRY. Nay, lavish not thy love on me. (*Crosses to R., behind Desmond*) There is another worthier far. (*Hits him with bladder*)

BEAUTY. Who is this suitor, boy?

WICKED FAIRY. His name, Desmonio. (*Bumps Desmond, who moves C. Sits on floor over R.*)

BEAUTY.
Desmonio. It is a name which doth
Make music of a moan. I'll to him straight.
(*Takes step R.*)

DESMOND.
But straighter he to thee.

BEAUTY.
                  Desmonio,
How is thy name lullabied upon my tongue,
And bathed in breath as sweet as roses' scent!

DESMOND. (*Crossing in to her, puts arm around her*)
   The name is not enough. The man must follow.

BEAUTY. (*Seeing him*)
   Art thou Desmonio, then?

DESMOND. (*Moving back*)
   The same.

BEAUTY.
   How I have wronged thee! Thy eagerness deceived.
   O sweet Desmonio, now I am invaded
   With a love that knows no satisfaction.

DESMOND.
   Let's to't, then.
   (*Takes her in his arms. Starts L. Good Fairy enters L., dressed as an Illyrian nun*)

GOOD FAIRY. For shame! (*Desmond puts Beauty down, as Good Fairy lifts her veil*)

DESMOND. (*Crossing R.C.*) The Illyrian Nun! (*Kneels on floor*)

BEAUTY. (*Looks at her, shrieks*)
   It is my mother! All's ill wi' me!
   (*Falls to her knees at R. of Good Fairy. Wicked Fairy pounds bladder on floor, jumping up and down, shouting "No! No! No!" Curtain of inner stage falls*)

WESLEY. Dammit, Aimé, I didn't get that. Gee, we seem to talk the same language, Des and I—at least we use the same words—we both talk American—English, whatever you like to call it—and yet, well, I guess I understood more about your motivations than I did about his.

AIMÉ. (*Crossing to Wesley*) Perhaps we French know them

better than you do . . . you are such recent friends, while we and the English are such old enemies.

WESLEY. I don't understand. I go for that girl in a big way, Aimé. (*Turns away R.*) The way I see her when I shut my eyes, I could just crush her (*Hugs himself*) to me and whisper—oh, and there'd be music, real sweet and soft—and I'd tell her—make her see things my way, that we're meant for one another, that life's wonderful, and deep and real.

AIMÉ. The English are never so direct.

WESLEY. How do you mean?

AIMÉ. The English gaze at their countryside through a swirl of pipe-smoke, through the sights of a huntsman's gun, from under wet umbrellas, and they link all generations in their mind. History is a reality, for the gigantic oaks are living witnesses of it. The cliffs were already there to echo the trumpets of long-forgotten battles, while the mansions are but sleeping-quarters for the dead. The supernatural holds no surprises for them in the sacred preserves in which they wander with such unspoken relish. Only the present, the realistic commonplace, shocks them, and they are driven to embarrassed silence by the events of every day. That is the reason why you, Ikonenko, are so profoundly shocking to them.

IKONENKO. I fail to see why I should be profoundly shocking.

AIMÉ. That's your charm, my friend. (*Wicked Fairy looks through C. curtains*)

WICKED FAIRY. Two down, two to go. Next, please.

WESLEY. (*Turns U. to Wicked Fairy*) O.K., I'm ready.

WICKED FAIRY. Just for your impatience, I shall put you last.

WESLEY. That's unfair. That's victimization! (*Crosses R.*)

IKONENKO. (*Rises, crosses D.L.*) Let him go. I do not wish to take part in the experiment.

AIMÉ. (*A step toward Ikonenko*) What?

WICKED FAIRY. Don't you love the girl?

IKONENKO. What is the meaning of such a word? Is it a realistic approach to life to say that you are at any time in love?

WESLEY. Oh, hell. Can't you forget your damned realism for a moment?

IKONENKO. No, because I am dialectically mature. People who have never seen a bath do not want a bath. That is realistic. Knowledge breeds desire, and desire breeds hatred.

WICKED FAIRY. (*Sly*) Yes, but you have seen the girl. You know her.

IKONENKO. Unfortunately.

WICKED FAIRY. Those flaxen curls, that freckled face, those strong arms and legs, that healthy, child-bearing body. Can you resist it?

IKONENKO. (*After a pause*) I shall go to see her again. For no other reason. (*Crosses onto stage L.*)

WICKED FAIRY. Which period do you wish to see her in?

IKONENKO. A period in which they had the rounded epaulettes with tassels on them. (*Exits L.*)

WICKED FAIRY. (*Smiling*) Very well. Orchestra! A Valse Pathétique! (*Orchestra begins to play a sentimental waltz. Wicked Fairy exits. Desmond returns from L., back in uniform*)

DESMOND. (*Crosses D. forestage to L.C.*) I say, was I awfully embarrassing? I mean, did I let a lot of cats out of the proverbial bag?

AIMÉ. Quite enough. Do you write poetry?

DESMOND. (*Embarrassed*) Oh, that. Just for fun. Not seriously.

AIMÉ. Like so many English, you are permanently embarrassed.

DESMOND. There's so damned much to be embarrassed about.

WESLEY. Have you ever published a poem? (*Steps toward Desmond*)

DESMOND (*Laughs softly*) Yes, I have. Twice. Once in the *Observer*, the other time in *Country Life*. I took a woman's name to write both—thought they'd have a better chance. I was right.

WESLEY. (*Shocked*) A woman's name!

DESMOND. It doesn't do to have a Colonel writing about trees and flowers, not in England—not on the active list.

AIMÉ. Desmond, you amaze me. I have often watched you, and I think I know you a little better now. God forbid, you will say. You don't really want to be known.

DESMOND. (*Embarrassed*) I don't mind.

WESLEY. Hey, what's all this talk about nuns? An Illyrian nun?

DESMOND. (*Wincing*) An Illyrian nun . . . Oh, nothing. I just behaved rather disgracefully to a Yugoslav girl when I was there.

84　THE LOVE OF FOUR COLONELS

WESLEY. A nun?

DESMOND. No. no. Just a girl. A young girl. I let her down. It was a caddish thing to do. Did I refer to her as a nun?

WESLEY. Yes.

DESMOND. Well, it just shows what the conscience will do to force its way into the imagination. *(Aimé and Wesley say in unison, "Uh-huh!")*

AIMÉ. *(As Wesley crosses L.)* The romantic imagination.

DESMOND. *(Turning)* Oh, for heaven's sake, leave romance to Wesley.

WESLEY. *(Crossing to box, sits on U. chair, Aimé on C. chair)* Yeah, yeah, leave romance to me! Just leave it to me . . . *(Aimé and Desmond exchange looks. The lights dim. Curtain rises to reveal a Chekhovian garden. Croquet hoops on ground. Beauty, dressed in 1900 costume, and stouter than before, is idly playing croquet. Ikonenko wears dark-green uniform with epaulettes; sits on a garden swing, and is knitting a red mitten)*

IKONENKO. So it is summer once again . . . who would have thought it?

BEAUTY. Summer seems to pass like a single hour when one is playing croquet . . . Anatol Lvovitch will be thirty-eight next birthday . . . *(Hits croquet ball to off R. Pause)*

IKONENKO. Excuse me, Aurora Petrovna, I have not been listening to what you have been saying . . .

BEAUTY. It was nothing . . .

IKONENKO. It was something . . . it was something. . . . "Golden words tumble from your lips like a waterfall lit by the midnight sun" . . . that was Pushkin, I believe . . . great man, Pushkin. Greatest poet Russia ever had.

BEAUTY. I don't read . . .

IKONENKO. None of us read. You play croquet . . . I knit . . . I am knitting a pair of mittens for Kolya, the medical orderly. . . . Why do we do it?

BEAUTY. Are we in love?

IKONENKO. In love?

BEAUTY. It is so important not to give up hope. (*She hits croquet ball with her mallet. Points to R.*) There, I have scored a splendid point, (*Turns, looks at him*) and there was nobody here to see it. (*Sits in chair. Pause. A shot rings out*) What was that?

IKONENKO. A woodman felling a birch tree . . .

BEAUTY. It sounded to me like . . .

IKONENKO. It was raining in Kharkov last Friday. I know, because Grischa left his umbrella at the barracks.

BEAUTY. Ever since Papa died, I have never carried an umbrella. There were so many at the funeral . . .

IKONENKO. Was it raining?

BEAUTY. No . . . (*Pause. Ikonenko looks at knitting*)

IKONENKO. Now I have dropped a stitch, and must undo it all. (*Does so*)

BEAUTY. (*Rises, crosses D. a step or two*) I was so looking forward to yesterday.

IKONENKO. Sadovsky's dance?

BEAUTY. Yes . . . but now that it is over, I cannot look forward to it any more . . .

IKONENKO. I did not go . . .

BEAUTY. Neither did I . . .

IKONENKO. I stayed here . . . in the drawing room . . . mending the General's watch . . .

BEAUTY. I was here, too . . . in the dining room . . . thinking . . .

IKONENKO. We were in the house alone . . .

BEAUTY. Yes . . .

IKONENKO. Hmpf! And I never knew . . . (*Wicked Fairy enters L., dressed in eccentric summer clothes, and with a long white beard*)

WICKED FAIRY. (*Crossing to C.*) Whoo-ooh! Do I interrupt a love feast? Are the love-birds ruthlessly pecking one another? . . . Have I chanced upon a courtship in the aviary?

BEAUTY. (*Crossing C. to him*) Dear darling Uncle!

WICKED FAIRY. Is my starling playing croquet, then? Ah, but only until evening, I'll warrant? Eh? Then when the moon emerges from her starry retreat—? (*Crosses L. Business of legs and arms. Goes behind swing, arms about Ikonenko, humming "Volga Boat Song"*) Eh? Eh? Do I make myself clear?

IKONENKO. I must leave for Moscow tonight.

BEAUTY. (*Turns away to front*) Tonight?

AMERICAN SCENE

photo by John Erwin

photo by John Erwin

OFFICE SCENE

ELIZABETHAN SCENE

photo by John Erwin

photo by Fred Fehl

RUSSIAN SCENE

THE LOVE OF FOUR COLONELS 87

IKONENKO. (*Wicked Fairy puts ear trumpet to his ear. Ikonenko shouts into it*) They have given me a regiment in Kazakstan.

WICKED FAIRY. (*Crossing C.*) What a disgrace! (*Blows trumpet*) How you have upset me! There is no telling what the authorities will do.

BEAUTY. Dear, dear Uncle! (*Goes to Wicked Fairy, to lead him to chair*)

WICKED FAIRY. All the same, it has excited me somewhat. (*Crosses to chair R.*) I really must sit down. (*Pretends to shoot into the air with an imaginary gun*) Piff! Paff! Pouf! (*Sits in armchair. Beauty kneels before him*) I enjoy shooting seagulls, but it is less cruel without a gun. (*Looks at her*) What pretty flowers! Stunted rhododendrons. You really should water your hat more often. (*Shot rings out*)

BEAUTY. There is that noise again . . . there cannot be many birch trees left . . . my poor, lovely birch trees . . .

WICKED FAIRY. That's no birch tree. It is Uncle Mischa trying to shoot himself. It really is degrading how he fails at everything he puts his hand to. So bad for the family's name.

BEAUTY. (*Still kneeling*) Why does Uncle Mischa do it?

WICKED FAIRY. He is in love . . .

BEAUTY. (*Rising, a step D. stage*) With life . . . like me?

WICKED FAIRY. (*Rises, crosses L.*) He is in love, and at least he does something about it. He doesn't just sit there knitting— (*Pushes swing in which Ikonenko is sitting U.R.*)

IKONENKO. Purl one, drop two. (*Pause. Suddenly Wicked Fairy, furious, tears off his wig, and pushes his false beard up onto his forehead*)

WICKED FAIRY. (*To Ikonenko, out of character—moves away from swing, which moves L. to R. two or three times*) Damn it! You're just not trying!

IKONENKO. Why should I try? Haven't I seen what happened to the others?

WICKED FAIRY. I give you one last chance. Will you seduce her, or not?

IKONENKO. No! (*Good Fairy enters L., comes L.C. She is much stouter than before. She is dressed from head to foot in black*)

GOOD FAIRY. (*Crossing in C.*) D'you mean to say I've got dressed up for nothing?

IKONENKO. Aha! You are my wife. I knew you would come if I tried to seduce her. What's the use?

BEAUTY. (*Who has been idling with croquet mallet*) What's the use? (*Hits ball to off R.*)

WICKED FAIRY. What's the use? (*Curtain of inner stage falls. Wicked Fairy puts head through curtain, exits.*) Next, please. Colonel Breitenspiegel.

WESLEY. (*Crossing R. toward Wicked Fairy*) At last! Just you watch me.

DESMOND. (*Rising*) I'll wish you good luck now.

WESLEY. You don't have to, brother. You're crazy—all of you. I'm amazed, honestly. You've got a chance to pick the girl of your dreams, and you go for the damnedest collection of dames I ever saw. Hell, she's got to have sex. She's got to be all right, and normal, and give you butterflies in the stomach just to look at her. I can see her now. Boy!

THE LOVE OF FOUR COLONELS

AIMÉ. And I can see from your expression that I will find her insupportable.

WESLEY. (*Moves toward Aimé—hostile*) Don't you say a word against her.

DESMOND. He hasn't seen her yet, old man.

WESLEY. (*Toward Aimé*) All the same, I didn't like the way he said that.

WICKED FAIRY. (*Head through curtains*) What period would you like her in?

WESLEY. (*To Wicked Fairy*) What periods are there? (*With a look of disgust at them, Wicked Fairy leaves C. curtain*)

DESMOND. American Civil War.

WESLEY. Hell, no! Those damn crinolines get in the way.

AIMÉ. The Roaring Twenties. (*Wicked Fairy puts head through C. curtain*)

WESLEY. I've had enough of you, friend.

WICKED FAIRY. Come, come, make up your mind.

WESLEY. I'll see her—

DESMOND. In a space-ship.

AIMÉ. In Hollywood.

WESLEY. (*To Wicked Fairy*) Leave that to me, will you, feller?

WICKED FAIRY. (*As he exits*) Will you join me, now, please?

WESLEY. (*Strides out onto upper stage L., elated*) Sure. Well, this is it. (*Shakes hands with himself over his head. As Wesley exits L., Ikonenko enters R., crosses D. onto forestage*)

DESMOND. Damn clever, you were.

IKONENKO. (*Crossing R.C.*) I was practical, and materialistic. I adjusted myself to the circumstances. The Revolution of 1905 failed because its intentions were clear to the enemy. Lenin did not make the same mistake in 1917.

DESMOND. (*Crossing C. to Ikonenko*) But why did you choose a pre-revolutionary period?

IKONENKO. Because we are now reconciled to the immediate past. I am now in a position to admit that the Czarist regime, while corrupt and loathsome, was still a Russian regime, and therefore neither so loathsome nor corrupt as it would have been had it not been Russian.

AIMÉ. (*Out of box, crossing L. of Desmond*) But you spoke with affection of the old style of epaulettes.

IKONENKO. I admit that they have always attracted me artistically, because they were big and heavy.

AIMÉ. (*Crossing Desmond to Ikonenko*) Do you criticize the new epaulettes?

IKONENKO. No. I criticize myself for preferring the old ones.

DESMOND. What are your feelings about chain-mail armor?

IKONENKO. My opinions on chain-mail armor have never been formulated, and if they were they would not be made public. (*Desmond crosses below Ikonenko R. Aimé and Desmond smile at one another. Ikonenko crosses R.*) In what period has our American friend decided to appear?

THE LOVE OF FOUR COLONELS 91

DESMOND. He wouldn't say. I had hopes of the American Civil War.

IKONENKO. No. Wall Street.

AIMÉ. That's probably more like it. I mistrust people who boast of their romanticism.

WICKED FAIRY. (*Looking through curtains*) Music. Cacophany! (*Orchestra plays a highly sentimental blues*) Chamberlain, no footlights this time. (*Disappears from curtain*)

AIMÉ. That sounds promising. (*Crosses into box, sits in D. chair*)

DESMOND. (*Crossing into box R.*) Donovan's still up there, I notice.

IKONENKO. (*Crossing into box R., sits in C. chair*) She has understood the full measure of Carabosse's duplicity.

DESMOND. Here we go. (*Curtain rises on the outline of a honkytonk bar. Beauty is standing under lamp-post outside, an unmistakable streetwalker. She gazes out with the idealized melancholy of her profession*) Good gracious!

IKONENKO. (*Rising*) This is an outrage!

AIMÉ. Sit down, sit down. Wait for the hero of fiction. (*Desmond sits in U.R. chair in box R. Beauty enters room, prances to bar R.*) Here he comes . . . (*Wesley enters dressed as a clergyman as she sits at bar. Crosses to chair R. of table L., sits*)

DESMOND. I say, he told me his greatest ambition was to lead the Charge of the Light Brigade.

AIMÉ. You took us by surprise, Desmond. You must allow him the same privilege. (*Beauty crosses L. below Wesley, sits L. of table. Wesley offers her a cigarette, and as she crosses him, she hums a song in a low voice as she crosses L.)*

WESLEY. Cigarette? *(Silence)*

BEAUTY. Are you talking to me?

WESLEY. *(Looking around)* Yeah, I guess I was.

BEAUTY. If you want me, I'll give you a price. I don't go for opening gambits.

WESLEY. *(With self-righteous smile)* I don't . . . er . . . want you. I was offering you a cigarette.

BEAUTY. *(Incredulous)* For free?

WESLEY. Sure.

BEAUTY. *(Staggered)* Hey, what kind of a fellow are you?

WESLEY. Can't you see?

BEAUTY. Yeah, I can see. I got eyes. *(She takes cigarette, he lights it)* Listen, you oughta be in church. This is no place for you.

WESLEY. You're wrong. This is for me, and it's you ought to be right there in church, child.

BEAUTY. Yeah? Where d'you get that "child" from?

WESLEY. We are all—

BEAUTY. I know. God's kids. I got loaded with that baloney at Sunday School. *(Crosses to C.)*

WESLEY. *(Laughing)* We're going to have quite a time putting *you* right, my dear.

THE LOVE OF FOUR COLONELS 93

BEAUTY. (*At his R.*) If you want to keep that smile on yer kisser, you better not try, on account of I don't want to be put right, my dear. (*Crosses to bar*)

WESLEY. You haven't told me your name.

BEAUTY. Want my telephone number, too?

WESLEY. No, no, no, no. I'm Father Breitenspiegel. They call me the Fighting Father.

BEAUTY. (*Impressed*) Hey, are you Fighting Father Breitenspiegel? *The* Fighting Father Breitenspiegel?

WESLEY. Sure. The guy that started Girls' Town.

BEAUTY. Well!

WESLEY. Now will you tell me your name?

BEAUTY. (*Crosses in C.*) Aurora-Mae Duckworth.

WESLEY. (*Rises, crosses to C.*) Aurora-Mae. Kinda cute name.

BEAUTY. They call me Rory.

WESLEY. Who's "they"?

BEAUTY. Guys.

WESLEY. Which guys?

BEAUTY. (*Crosses D.L. to below L. chair*) How do I know? I only see them once.

WESLEY. (*Crossing in L.C.*) Listen, Rory, I want you to know something.

BEAUTY. Something I don't know? (*Giggles, sits in chair L.*)

WESLEY. Sure. The world's not like you think it is. (*Sits beside her*)

BEAUTY. The world's tough like last week's steak.

WESLEY. I want to take you away from here, Rory, but bad.

BEAUTY. (*Leaning over table*) Why don't you shut up?

WESLEY. Rory, ever seen the sun rise over the Alleghenies? It comes up like a great big lantern in the sky, and seems to say, "Get up, get up" to all God's creatures. "I'm back again, folks," it says (*Rises*), "I've been keeping guys warm right to the other side of the great wide world." (*Crosses behind table, stands*) And you'd kneel there, Rory, filling your canteen by the brook, and say to it, "Thanks, sun, it's sure good to see you back. You're a pal." (*Crosses to juke-box*) And the old sun 'ud say, "Don't thank me, Rory, I'm doing my duty—are you?" (*Goes behind juke-box, his hands on it as a preacher uses his pulpit*) And you'd think, and smile up at him, and say, "Sure, Mr. Sun, I've left the city lights way back of me. It's my turn to build up the bonfire for breakfast at Girls' Town." "What's cookin', kids?" he'll call. (*Sits in chair R. of table*) "Waffles with maple syrup, ham and eggs, cornflakes, and real good coffee." Then, if it rains, Rory, you'll know that it's just the poor old fellow's mouth watering.

AIMÉ. I have an irresistible desire to brush my teeth. (*Wicked Fairy starts on from L. to U.C. Enters, crosses to bar*)

BEAUTY. (*Visibly moved*) I'm sorry, Father—you're too late. (*Door opens, and Wicked Fairy enters, dressed as a gangster. His face is practically concealed in the upturned collar of his overcoat, beneath which can be seen the striped trousers of a convict*) Hey! Just go on talking to me, that's all.

THE LOVE OF FOUR COLONELS

WESLEY. What's wrong?

BEAUTY. Please. Pretend to know me.

WESLEY. Who is that guy, Rory? (*Wicked Fairy bangs on bar*)

WICKED FAIRY. Don't I get any service around here? (*At bar*)

BEAUTY. (*Urgent—pulls hair over face, turns away to L.*) Don't answer!

WICKED FAIRY. Anybody got ears?

WESLEY. (*Crossing R. to Wicked Fairy*) Why, yes—*I* have.

WICKED FAIRY. (*Swinging around*) No kiddin'! Then keep them shut, if you know what's good. (*Pushes Wesley against jukebox. Smirks, crossing C.*) Hiya, Rory. You didn't figure you'd see me again so soon, huh?

BEAUTY. What are you doing here? You got a ninety-nine-year stretch.

WICKED FAIRY. I came out on parole, honey, just to see you.

WESLEY. (*Crossing D.R.*) Say, didn't I see your face in the newspaper? You're Tony Carabosse. You didn't come out on parole. You broke jail.

WICKED FAIRY. (*Crosses to R. to Wesley*) O.K., wise guy. So I granted myself parole. What's the difference?

WESLEY. Why, that's illegal!

WICKED FAIRY. (*To Beauty*) Hey, what kind of brainy guys are you going with these days, sugar? (*Laughs, crosses a bit to C.*)

BEAUTY. What do you want, Tony?

WICKED FAIRY. *(Continues cross to table, sits)* I want to settle a little argument we never finished, baby. Remember the time the cops came, and you kept going to the window, said you felt hot? Sure you felt hot, you dirty, double-crossing she-dog. Yeah. *(Pulls out revolver, points it at her)*

WESLEY. Put that gun away.

WICKED FAIRY. Button your lip. *(Points revolver at Wesley)*

WESLEY. Have you a license for that firearm?

WICKED FAIRY. Sure, bishop, I even got a diploma.

BEAUTY. You wouldn't dare shoot me! *(Rises)*

WICKED FAIRY. No?

WESLEY. You'd be guilty of first-degree murder.

WICKED FAIRY. You're wrong, saint, I got me a good mouthpiece. I never get more than second degree.

WESLEY. You will this time!

WICKED FAIRY. How come?

WESLEY. *(C.)* I'll be right there in the courtroom.

WICKED FAIRY. *(Rises, crosses C., works U., to juke-box, as Wesley faces toward bar)* You'll be a patch of grass, brother. I'll pump you both full of lead. A guy can't die twice, and if I go, you're coming right along with me. *(Bumps into juke-box U.R.C. It plays—he jumps away from it toward C. Turns, looks at it, shoots it. It stops. Pause. Wicked Fairy crosses, sits down on table)* Yeah, funny thing. I'm in a generous mood. Give you one more chance, sugar, and then it's curtains. I figure I've got to that time in a guy's life when he kinda wants something different, something solid. Listen, babe, I'm goin' straight.

WESLEY. You're going straight?

WICKED FAIRY. Sure, after I've bumped you off I'm goin' straight. I'm gonna run a gambling ship off the coast of Yucatan—strictly on the level. I got dough—plenty dough. A guy don't live forever.

WESLEY. He may inherit the life everlasting.

WICKED FAIRY. Don't give me that, will ya!

BEAUTY. Yeah—don't give us that, will ya!

WICKED FAIRY. Listen, babe, I wanna kid—a kid can take over the gambling ship when I'm cold. (*Reaches out his leg, encircles Beauty, pulls her to him with his leg*)

BEAUTY. (*Frees herself, pushing his leg away*) Are you suggesting marriage?

WICKED FAIRY. (*Rises, crosses a step C.*) Don't say it that way, it don't sound so good.

BEAUTY. (*Takes his L. arm, turns him to her*) Listen, louse. I go with guys, but I don't marry them. That's not me. I'm not made that way. That's not the way I tick. (*Crosses R.C.*) I'm one of the little people, that like little, simple things. I'm little, and I like little guys, guys that go to the ball game Sundays and stand right there and shout and put their souls into their shouting. I don't want big ideas, Tony Carabosse, on account of they eat you up, like fire, from the inside. It's guys like you try to smash the little things, and the beautiful deep things, and the U.S. Constitution.

IKONENKO. Has she refused?

BEAUTY. (*Crossing D.L.—vastly superior*) And there's something else. Thomas Jefferson once said—

WICKED FAIRY. (*Breathing*) O.K., sister. You asked for this. (*He is about to shoot, when Wesley expertly knocks gun out of his hand, and confiscates it. Throws Wicked Fairy to bar*)

WESLEY. Stay where you are.

WICKED FAIRY. (*Quavering*) Don't do it! Don't shoot me! I'll give you a partnership in the gambling hall, Reverend. Fifty grand down, and I'll pay your taxes.

WESLEY. Why, you poor misguided child. I'm going to call the District Attorney, but first—

WICKED FAIRY. They got dames in Mexico. Swell dames. And dough.

WESLEY. (*Louder*) But first—

WICKED FAIRY. Liquor. Automobiles . . .

WESLEY. (*Shouting*) But first, I'm going to teach you a little Scripture lesson.

WICKED FAIRY. (*Falling to his knees*) Oh, no—not that!

WESLEY. Sure. (*Holds revolver toward Wicked Fairy*) Samson smote the Philistine host with the jawbone of an ass, and slew a thousand men therewith. I'm not that ambitious. I'll take them on one at a time. (*Throws down revolver to L. After a moment of indecision, Wicked Fairy makes a dive for it. Wesley is too quick for him, seizes him, lifts him into the air. Wicked Fairy, being upstage, places his feet on Wesley's stomach and shoves him off to over R. Wicked Fairy crosses D.L. The fight is on. As it starts, Beauty pushes revolver under table with her foot, crosses U.L.C. Wesley knocks Wicked Fairy out, and*

Wicked Fairy falls to ground. One writhe, and all is stillness. Beauty awaits his embrace)

BEAUTY. (*Crosses in*) O.K., feller, you win. When do we leave for Girls' Town?

WESLEY. Then you'll come?

BEAUTY. You've been fighting over me, haven't you?

WESLEY. I wasn't fighting just for you, Rory, but for the forces of light and freedom all over the world.

BEAUTY. (*Seductive—throws arms round his neck*) That's as may be, but it's me you want.

WESLEY. (*Powerful*) I have come to save you from the abyss, not to be dragged down myself!

BEAUTY. (*Steps away from him—sadly*) You got me wrong, butch. I never lived like this. This is my first day's work.

WESLEY. (*Foolishly radiant*) Then I have saved you! Saved you from blemish!

BEAUTY. That's the way it looks.

WESLEY. (*Earnest*) What do you want out of life, Aurora-Mae?

BEAUTY. (*Much too fierce*) I want a guy I can *respect*!

WESLEY. (*Jaw rippling. Exaggeratedly manly*) I'm crazy about you, Rory, you must know that. I want you to marry me.

BEAUTY. But—? (*Looks at his collar*)

WESLEY. I know what you're thinking. Listen, my dear . . . they only call me "Father." I'm an Episcopalian.

BEAUTY. (*Falls on his neck*) Whoopee! Hold me tight. Tighter. (*Her eyes shut in ecstasy*) My holy dreamboat! My Noah's Ark! (*They are about to kiss when Good Fairy enters U.C., bespectacled and grim. She crosses L.C.*)

GOOD FAIRY. So there you are, Wesley Breitenspiegel.

WESLEY. (*Agonized, as he breaks away from Beauty*) Why do you follow me around?

GOOD FAIRY. Now come away from that girl, Wesley, and just relax completely.

BEAUTY. Who is she? (*Grabs his coat collar, ready for disenchantment*) Is she your girl?

WESLEY. No.

BEAUTY. Your wife?

WESLEY. No. My psychiatrist. (*Beauty wails, crosses U.R.C., her back turned*)

WICKED FAIRY. Oh, Donovan, Donovan! (*Rising on his elbows*)

GOOD FAIRY. Carabosse—had enough? Curtain—bring it down! Curtain! (*Wicked Fairy is on his back, kicking his heels on floor*)

AIMÉ. (*Crossing C.*) Well, there is our great romantic!

DESMOND. (*Crossing R.C.*) You know, I'm going to find it awfully hard to work with you again after all this. (*Ikonenko crosses, D.R.*)

AIMÉ. Why, it may be easier. We can do amateur theatricals in the office every Wednesday. At least, we know each other's favorite periods. (*Good Fairy, smiling, comes through curtain, staying on platform*)

GOOD FAIRY. Well, what's your decision?

AIMÉ. What is there to decide? We have failed to seduce our Beauty, and that's that.

GOOD FAIRY. Thank God!

AIMÉ. (*Crossing L. of Good Fairy*) Why did you wish us to fail?

GOOD FAIRY. I wished you to fail because the Beauty belongs to me. She is my foothold in your hearts, in the hearts of all mankind. (*Wicked Fairy enters L. below curtains, crosses down to L. on forestage*)

WICKED FAIRY. More fine phrases! What about me? Was there ever a more annoying frustration than watching the Beauty, man's ideal, so nearly brought off her snow-white pedestal? (*Inner stage curtain falls. Wesley enters R., comes down on forestage*)

DESMOND. (*Turns to Wesley*) Bad luck, Galahad.

WICKED FAIRY. Bad luck! Donovan's damned interference. If you could have defiled the Beauty by the reality of a kiss, you would have been happy while cheating your wives, instead of sighing for something better. You would have taken to sin as the Devil takes to fire.

GOOD FAIRY. Now the Beauty will sleep unmolested for another hundred years.

WICKED FAIRY. (*Crossing U.L. on platform to C.*) Then I shall have more tricks up my sleeve—better ones, more compelling ones.

GOOD FAIRY. So shall I.

WICKED FAIRY. Don't you want to stay and try again?

DESMOND. Well, I'll tell you my decision. I'm going back. There's one thing you've overlooked in my case, you see. I'm quite fond of my wife. Not in any special way, you understand —that was over a long time ago, before I married her, to be precise. But I do want to see my dogs again—Ranger, Thunderbolt, and Black Havoc. And then . . . the editor of *Field* said he was interested in a poem for the Christmas issue—

IKONENKO. I too will return.

WICKED FAIRY. Why?

IKONENKO. Colonel Desmond is right. If we stayed, what would happen? We would wake again in a hundred years and try to seduce the Beauty again and again, and we would fail. Then we would return to life. I leave ideals to fools, and return to my duties as a Soviet officer with relief. Besides, I do not wish to forfeit my pension.

WICKED FAIRY. Colonel Frappot?

AIMÉ. The assessment of Colonel Ikonenko was surprisingly intelligent, if I may say so, and convincing to a materialist, but I am staying.

WICKED FAIRY. What! You do surprise me.

AIMÉ. I have lived my life as an explorer in the world of women. It has been easy, fascinating and often very beautiful, but it was all accessible and therefore transitory. All that I have not experienced is the quest for the unobtainable. My dear Fairies, you envy me the power to chose, but I am sick of choosing, for at the moment of choice I always regret what I have not done.

THE LOVE OF FOUR COLONELS

Therefore I long to give myself to the selfless and patient pursuit of a single elusive woman whom, as punishment, I shall never possess. (*Ends up D.L.*)

WICKED FAIRY. Bravo! —Colonel Breitenspiegel?

WESLEY. Well . . . I guess I'm staying, too. (*Crosses U.L.*) I sort of like the idea of waking up in a hundred years' time. I go for that. I would like to have another try at the Beauty, but even if I don't win her it will be great to look around in the year 2050 and see what the world is like. —Remember? I told you fellows I was a romantic at heart. (*Desmond crosses in box R., gets hat and gloves. Aimé and Wesley cross in box L., get hats and gloves. Ikonenko crosses in box R., gets hat*)

GOOD FAIRY. So, two of them are left behind unable to sin, unable to do good.

WICKED FAIRY. And two come back with us to join the throng on our eternal battleground.

GOOD FAIRY. And to think we nearly kissed!

WICKED FAIRY. Poor wretched goodness!

GOOD FAIRY. Poor benighted evil!

DESMOND. (*Crossing U.R.C.*) I hate to interrupt you, but are we leaving soon?

IKONENKO. (*Crossing R.C.*) I demand a safe passage to Headquarters.

GOOD FAIRY. (*Crossing to R. on platform*) Come away, Carabosse, let the others sleep. Come away back to the silly little muddled heads, the platforms, the bright lights and the slogans —come away—

WICKED FAIRY. Aimé, Wesley, go onto the stage now, please. (*Aimé and Wesley cross U.R. onto steps. Wesley goes U. on stage. Aimé pauses on steps*)

DESMOND. Any message to your wives?

WICKED FAIRY. That is not permitted. We will have to arrange an accident.

WESLEY. An accident?

WICKED FAIRY. Your disappearance will have to be explained. The police are so much more active than they were, even a hundred years ago. Chamberlain!

CHAMBERLAIN. (*Entering R.*) Yes, sir.

WICKED FAIRY. Two comfortable beds.

CHAMBERLAIN. (*Smiling feebly*) They're there, sir. —Er—I was going to ask you, sir.

WICKED FAIRY. Hmm?

CHAMBERLAIN. Could I come with you?

WICKED FAIRY. Come with me? Back to mortality? Why?

CHAMBERLAIN. (*Pathetic*) I want to die of old age in the mortal manner.

WICKED FAIRY. (*Livid*) Certainly not! You stay here!

GOOD FAIRY. Oh, Carabosse—

WICKED FAIRY. (*Passionately*) Why should he die when I can't? . . . Now. Say your farewells. (*Chamberlain, Good Fairy, and Wicked Fairy go off R. into wings*)

DESMOND. (*Crossing L.C.*) Good-bye, Aimé. I think you're mad.

AIMÉ. I enjoy taking myself by surprise. Bon voyage, Desmond, Sasha. (*He exits L. on platform*)

IKONENKO. (*Crossing L.*) Good-bye.

DESMOND. Good-bye, old son.

WESLEY. Pitch right in there, Des. Yahoo! (*Exits L. on platform*)

DESMOND. (*Crossing D.L.C.*) Extraordinary! Wesley is like a fellow with a great load off his mind. I say, you don't think we're being fools, leaving them?

IKONENKO. (*Crossing L.C.*) No.

DESMOND. We're not in any way letting them down . . . ? I'd hate to do that.

IKONENKO. We are right and they are wrong.

DESMOND. I hope so.

IKONENKO. (*Crossing L.*) I, too . . . (*Wicked Fairy and Good Fairy return from R. side of stage, dressed as a doctor and a nurse. Good Fairy follows Wicked Fairy, stops at R. end of platform*)

WICKED FAIRY. (*Entering R., crossing platform to L.*) Ideal clothes, you see. We'll arrive as a doctor and nurse straight from the scene of the accident. We'll have to put on grave faces, though.

IKONENKO. Mine is always grave. (*Exits L. after Desmond goes off L. Curtains part. The décor is the first pastoral setting, with two more beds, one on each side of Beauty. Aimé and Wesley are lying on them*)

WICKED FAIRY. Donovan—

GOOD FAIRY. (*Back to audience, crosses first to below Wicked Fairy, then to below Aimé*) Aimé, Wesley . . . sleep . . . a dreamless sleep . . .

WICKED FAIRY. Orchestra—sleep in five minutes—but until then, play! (*Good Fairy follows Wicked Fairy as far as box. Soft music begins. Wicked Fairy crosses down L. to L.*) Come on, no time to lose, back to the cold winds of the living world. (*Sees Chamberlain enter R., as he crosses to L.C. of stage*) As for you, just for your insolence I'll leave you here awake . . . awake for a hundred years! (*Chamberlain recoils in horror, crying, goes U. to L. a step, and sits*) Come on, come on, into the air . . . away . . . away . . . (*Ikonenko and Desmond have swept out. Exit Wicked Fairy D.L. His voice gets softer quickly. Chamberlain, on step, weeps. Good Fairy crosses U.L., lifts up Chamberlain*)

GOOD FAIRY. Come with me. We can't have you weeping here. I'm taking you with me, you wicked old man. (*Crosses down L.*)

CHAMBERLAIN. (*His face lighted up with hope*) Taking me with you?

GOOD FAIRY. Yes. I'm taking you to die as you want to . . . to teach you the meaning of charity. (*Exits L.*)

CHAMBERLAIN. Thank you . . . thank you . . . Oh, thank you . . . (*Chamberlain exits L. Pause. Aimé's and Wesley's two hands reach out and almost touch Beauty*)

WESLEY. (*Trying to touch her*) Aimé, I can't reach the Beauty . . . can you?

AIMÉ. (*Also trying to touch her*) No, not quite . . . it was arranged like this on purpose . . . (*Slight pause*)

WESLEY. Aimé.

AIMÉ. Mm?

WESLEY. Were we wrong not to go back?

AIMÉ. What is the use of asking such a question? At this precise moment they are asking themselves if *they* were wrong not to stay . . . (*Slight pause*) Wesley.

WESLEY. Mmm?

AIMÉ. (*Very drowsy*) I'm beginning to know the meaning of perfection.

WESLEY. Yeah . . . What is it? (*Music fades away. Snores from the sleepers*)

CURTAIN

PROPERTY AND FURNITURE PLOT

Act I, Scene 1
Office Scene

    6 office chairs
    1 large conference table
    2 smaller side tables
    Medium-size sofa
    Waste basket
    Filing cabinet
    Large table lamp
    Another (small) table light

    4 hats
    Cloak
    2 pairs gloves
    Cigars and matches
    2 magazines
    Seidlitz powders
    Glass of water
    Permit (official paper)
    Scroll (ancient document)
    Briefcase (Ikonenko) containing several documents
    Small pocket diary (Ikonenko)
    Fountain pens
    Small appointment book
    Pipe, tobacco and matches
    Small bell on table
    Tobacco pouch with tobacco
    Package of cigarettes
    Smelling salts in bottle
    Revolver and blank cartridge

Act I, Scene 2
Castle Scene

    Flashlight

Act I, Scene 3
Court Theater Scene in Castle (With Bed)

    Large bed with pillows, bedding

THE LOVE OF FOUR COLONELS

Act II
French Scene
- Dressing table
- Bench
- Love seat
- Hand mirror
- Lorgnette
- Wax taper

Act II
Elizabethan Scene
- Rock in foreground
- Knife
- Blown-up bladder

Act II
Russian Scene
- Swing
- Garden chair
- Croquet wickets
- Mallets and balls
- Knitting things
- Ear trumpet

Act II
American Scene
- Table
- 2 chairs
- Bar
- Stools
- Accessories for bar
- Cigarettes and matches
- Revolver and 2 blank cartridges
- 2 hats
- 2 pairs gloves

Act II
Court Theater in Castle
- 3 beds with pillows, bedding

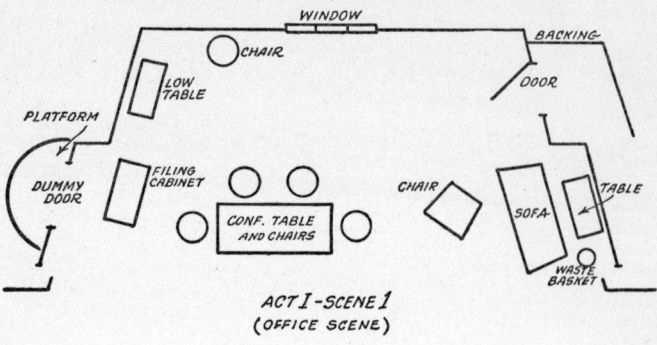

ACT I - SCENE 1
(OFFICE SCENE)

NOTE - - THE OFFICE AND FOREST SCENE, ACT I, SCENES 1 & 2 ARE THE ONLY ONES PLAYED ON THE REGULAR STAGE, PLUS THE INTERLUDES BETWEEN THE "CHARADES" AFTER THE SMALLER STAGE IS MOVED DOWN. THE FRONT AREA IS CALLED THE FORESTAGE.

THE SMALLER STAGE — ONCE IT HAS COME INTO POSITION, HAS A SMALL 1 FT. HIGH ORCHESTRA RAIL TO MASK A LOUD SPEAKER THROUGH WHICH MOST OF THE MUSIC COMES, IS PLACED UNDER THE RAIL.

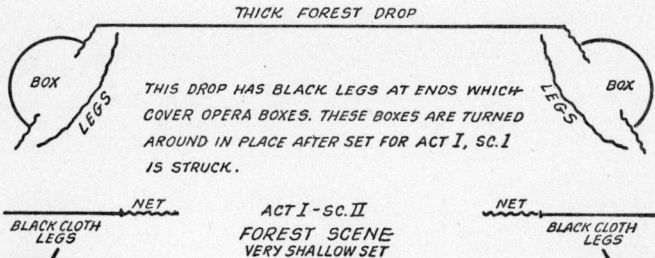

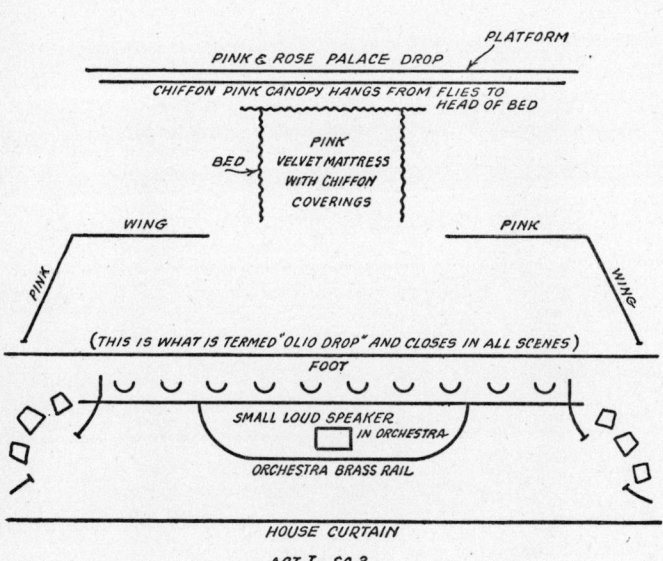

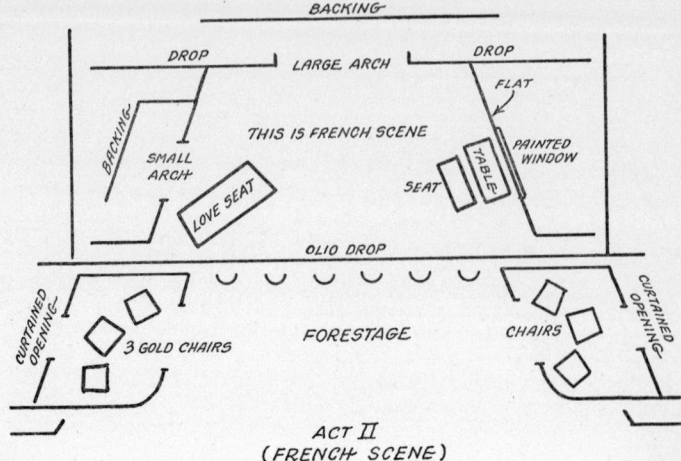

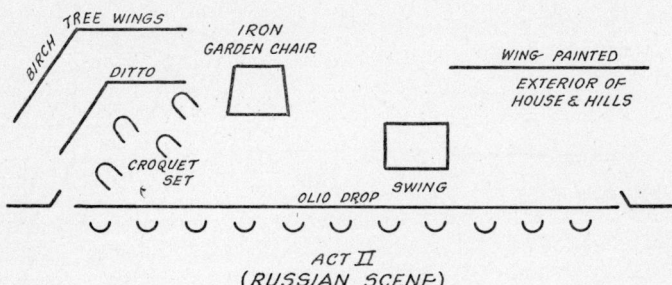

ACT II
(RUSSIAN SCENE)

ACT II
(AMERICAN SCENE)

Boston Public Library

**COPLEY SQUARE
GENERAL LIBRARY**

The Date Due Card in the pocket indicates the date on or before which
this book should be returned to the
Library.
Please do not remove cards from this
pocket.